D1882480

ANNUAL REPORT

OF THE

ARCHAEOLOGICAL SURVEY OF INDIA

1917-18

ANNUAL REPORT
OF THE
ARCHAEOLOGICAL SURVEY OF INDIA

1917-18

BY

Dr. D. B. SPOONER, Ph.D., F.A.S.B.
Officiating Director General of Archaeology in India

GYAN

Published by

Gyan Publishing House
5, Ansari Road
Daryaganj, New Delhi-110002
Phone: 011-47034999, 9811692060
E-mail: books@gyanbooks.com

Distribution Network
gyanbooks.com
India, USA, Canada, UK, Australia, France

© **Publisher**

All rights reserved. No part of this work may be reproduced, stored, adapted, or transmitted in any form or by any means, electronic, mechanical, photocopying, micro-filming, recording or otherwise, or translated in any language, without the prior written permission of the copyright owner and the publisher.

ISBN : 978-81-212-2502-1 (HB)
First Published, 1920

2nd Impression 2021

Printed at: Gyan Press, Delhi.

The book is sold subject to the condition that it shall not, by way of trade or otherwise, be lent, resold, hired out, or otherwise circulated without the prior publisher's written consent.

Annual Report of the
Archaeological Survey of India 1917-18
Author: Dr. D. B. Spooner

ANNUAL REPORT

OF THE

ARCHÆOLOGICAL SURVEY OF INDIA

1917-18.

BY

DR. D. B. SPOONER, Ph.D., F.A.S.B.
Officiating Director General of Archæology in India.

CALCUTTA
SUPERINTENDENT GOVERNMENT PRINTING, INDIA
1920

Price Rupees Two or Three shillings.

LIST OF PLATES.

LIST OF PLATES.

Annual Report of the Director-General of Archæology for the year 1917-18.

THE total sum of Rs. 3,04,816 was expended on the conservation of ancient monuments throughout British India in the year 1917-18. This figure is to be compared with Rs. 3,19,736 for the year preceding, but this latter figure itself represented a decrease of some Rs. 16,000 in the figures for 1915-16. It is hoped, however, that the downward tendency thus disclosed will be arrested, now that the War is happily over, and that normal expenditure will be both restored and maintained. There is no activity of Government to which the dictum that a "a stitch in time saves nine" is more applicable than to the upkeep of its ancient monuments. Even as it is, and despite the War, the falling off in most Provinces is very slight, while in some cases actual increases are shown, for example in the Delhi Province, with an expenditure of Rs. 59,940 in 1917-18 against Rs. 41,121 the year before; or the Central Provinces which this year records Rs. 13,432 against a previous Rs. 9,614. On the whole, therefore, it may be justly claimed that the policy of Government in regard to the preservation of those memorials of the past which it has inherited from its predecessors has been quite well maintained, considering the phenomenal difficulties of the last few years. Conservation.

As in previous years, repairs to the more important of the numerous memorials left by the Mughal and other Moslem dynasties preceding British Rule bulk largely in the year's activities, more than one third part of the entire expenditure on Conservation for this period having been devoted to this portion of the field.

Mr. Page, Superintendent Muhammadan and British Monuments, Agra, reports that a total sum of Rs. 1,26,644-4-2 was spent on conservation in his Circle alone this year, as compared with Rs. 1,12,712 in the previous year. In the United Provinces expenditure comes to Rs. 38,048-6-2; in the Punjab Rs. 28,655-14-0, and in the Delhi Province Rs. 59,940. But as Mr. Page states that of the long list of works taken in hand this season none presented any special feature such as to call for special care and attention on the part of the Public Works Department, beyond that normally demanded in such work, the following only need be mentioned in this place. Muhammadan and British Monuments.

(Conservation.) United Provinces

In the United Provinces the largest single estimate dealt with was one for Rs. 2,003-15-0 for work at the Bagh Khan-i-Alam in Agra. This is an old Mughal garden now badly ruined, and in use as a nursery in connexion with the Taj garden. The river front, which was dangerously dilapidated, has been put into a sound condition, and the further dilapidation of the west entrance gateway has been forestalled. At the Taj itself the only items of work this year were the shifting of the lamp-stands provided at the Taj forecourt (a measure entailed by an alteration in the approach road), and the removal of certain modern masonry watercourses formerly built along the edge of the causeways in the garden, so that now the original sides can be again exposed to view. At Mariam's tomb at Sikandara, a small sum was spent on refacing with red stone the steps leading down to the crypt chamber, and repaving the passage approach and the crypt chamber itself. Teak-wood doors of Mughal pattern were also provided here, and in response to a suggestion of the Hon'ble the Maharajadhiraja of Burdwan a low *jali* railing enclosing a space equal to and immediately above the actual grave in the crypt was affixed in a chamber on the ground floor with a view to prevent traffic over the actual spot of interment, a practice which was offensive to Indian religious sentiment. A sum of Rs. 521 was devoted to replacing a missing *chhajja*, refixing the fallen finials and generally refacing badly decayed stone at Bahau-d-din's tomb in Fatehpur Sikri. The structure is interesting historically as containing the grave of the person reputed to have been the architect of Akbar's palace, though an inscription in a mosque adjacent to his tomb refers to him more modestly as Daroga or Manager of the Imperial Chunam Works. The other items in this province though numerous were of too petty a nature to require detailed mention here.

Punjab.

The largest single work in the Punjab was in connexion with the Shalamar gardens at Lahore, where the enclosure wall, which had become dangerously undermined, was underpinned substantially throughout its length. The pavilion in the west wall in the centre of the first terrace was put into needed repair, and the bulged wall of the stair of the little Hammam in the east wall of the middle terrace was rebuilt. The *dalan* in the north wall of the third (lowest) terrace was reroofed, and a similar repair was undertaken on the little Sikh pavilion on the upper terrace. The repair of certain of the *Baradaries* and the causeways of the middle terrace about the central tank was necessitated through damage caused by the felling of the mango trees, preliminary to the layout of this terrace as a rose-garden. The expenditure in 1917-18 on these works is Rs. 4,582. At the Akbari serai an untidy cinder pathway laid around the enclosing *dalans* was removed at a cost of Rs. 737, the earth was dug up and a treatment of grassing carried right up to the face of the *dalans*. In the Lahore Fort the only work of special repair undertaken was in the little Sikh pavilion over the Shish Mahal, where the rotten wooden construction of the roof is being removed and replaced by rolled steel beams, which will however be hidden from view by the replacement of the original wooden ceiling. At the Haran Munara and Tank at Sheikhupura in the Gujranwala District, the southern *ghat*, which had collapsed, was rebuilt and the dilapidated portions of the parapet enclosing the tank were put into repair, while the remains of original plaster adhering to the central *Baradari* were secured. Hollows and low areas about the tank were made up with earth to permit of the proper drainage of the area, to the lack of which some of the damage referred to above was primarily due. Accumulated silt was also removed from the lower terraces of the tank. The bulk of these works were begun in 1916 and carried to completion in the year under report. At Ramnagar in the Gujranwala District a small sum was spent in connexion with the setting up of a memorial tablet and masonry pillar at the grave of Subedar Major Mir Sher Ali, Sardar Bahadur, of the 8th Light Cavalry, Bengal Native Army, to commemorate the heroism of this old man, who, when 78 years of age, fell in the battle of Ramnagar on 22nd November 1848 against the Sikhs. Petty repair was also effected to the Takht-i-Akbari at Kalanaur in Gurdaspur District, where the floor of the *chabutra* was made good. This monument is of interest as being the site of Akbar's coronation prior to his return to the capital on 14th February 1556 on the news of the death of his father Humayun. (Conservation.)

Thirty-three estimates for special repairs were dealt with in the Delhi Province during the year, of which four related to works in connexion with Humayun's tomb in Delhi. The question of an appropriate lay out of the enclosing garden to this monument was taken up and a scheme prepared in consultation with the Superintendent, Arboricultural Operations, Delhi. This is now being put into effect as far as the adverse conditions engendered by a very brackish soil and water-supply permit. Tests are to be taken with a view to the provision, if possible, of a sweet water supply. But until the solution of this problem is arrived at, it is feared that little real progress can be hoped for. A wooden gateway was provided to the small doorway in the north wall of the enclosure, and a low one-strand railing was erected along the path approach between Bu Halima Garden and the west entrance gateway to prevent traffic over the grass plots at the sides. A separate estimate provided for rebuilding the portions of the enclosing wall of the garden at the south-west corner and again to the immediate south of the entrance gate, and a further estimate provided for four more red stone seats of appropriate design which were set up on the main *chabutra* above the mausoleum for the convenience of visitors. At the Qila Kohna Masjid in Purana Qila, the forecourt was also laid out with grass and biota trees, accentuating the original features of the small enclosure, and a further small estimate provided for laying out a pathway from the central circus direct to the Qila Kohna mosque. As regards the Purana Qila itself further work in connexion with the grassing and planting of the interior with trees was undertaken to the amount of Rs. 3,261 during the year under review. But the principal works at Purana Qila in this year, for which an estimate of Rs. 6,819 had been drawn up, comprised the building up of a great gap in the south wall where the old work—here of a very *kachcha* nature—had collapsed, endangering the safety of adjacent portions. The treatment here was on the most economical lines possible, a *pakka* stone-in-lime facing averaging some 3 feet in depth being erected to a height of 20 feet from the ground. The portion above was dealt with by stone flagging laid to a one-in-one slope to secure it from the effects of rain water. A low breast wall has (Delhi.)

(Conservation.) also been built along the top of this flagged slope to prevent persons from falling over the edge. A good deal of underpinning and pointing was also carried out where urgently needed in other places around the walls exteriorly, while in the continuous surrounding *dalans* on the inner face of the walls much was also done in this way to preserve the remains of this interesting feature of the citadel. Two separate estimates were dealt with in securing against further dilapidation the badly ruined bastions at the north-west and south-west corners of the citadel, a similar treatment of wall-facing at the base and stone flagging above. being adopted here also. At the Humayun Gate great mounds of débris resulting from the demolition and clearance of the village huts were cleared away at a cost of Rs. 648, and a path was cut to descend to the level of the *bela* below. A few remaining fragments of original paving were disclosed towards the top in the course of this clearance. In the west wall again, facing the Delhi-Muttra Road, a small walled-up postern was opened out, and an original vaulted passage-way through the thickness of the wall was revealed. Curiously, no trace of a stair or any means of ascent to the upper level of the citadel came to light, and the excavation will be kept open by ramping back the earth to the upper level of the interior, and providing a narrow flight of steps for access from above. A further estimate of Rs. 4,238 was provided for securing the remains of the underground water pavilion near the Sher Mandal inside the citadel, a structure first disclosed to view in 1913 on the demolition and clearance of village huts which formerly crowded this area. At Hauz Khas, a footpath between this group of monuments and the end of the raised *band* approach was made for the convenience of visitors, and some small repairs of urgent nature were undertaken at the north-west and south-east ends of the *dalans* along the sides of the tank. At Firozshah Kotla only two minor repairs have to be recorded, the construction of a surface drain, and the repair of a gateway on the river front. In Delhi city (Shahjahanabad) a simple iron railing was erected across the top of the breach made in the Water Bastion in the assault of Delhi in 1857, to prevent people from falling over from above, a railing of this nature having the advantage of not altering the original appearance of the breach. In the Delhi Fort some minor alterations in the design of the stone water-channels and the causeway in the Hayat Bakhsh garden were carried out to permit of their being more easily crossed by visitors, while in the Diwan-i-Khas the repair of a fractured panel of the inlaid dado of one of the piers was taken in hand. In the Qudsia garden the ruined late Mughal mosque was secured against further dilapidation at a cost of Rs. 817, and Rs. 1,350 were expended on the conservation of the Lal Darwaza, a gate of old Delhi Sher Shahi near the jail. At Tripolia—mile 2¼ on the Delhi-Karnal Road—some useful repair in the nature of underpinning was undertaken upon the southern gateway of the now fallen serai, while the old mosque near Mahabat Khan's Haveli on the Delhi-Muttra Road was secured against threatened collapse, the cost amounting to Rs. 978. At the Qutb, a new buttress was erected to replace a fallen one in support of the south-east corner of the original mosque of Qutbu-d-Din, and certain portions of the late Mughal serai at the entrance to the Qutb grounds, which had fallen during the rains, were rebuilt. The largest single estimate in the Qutb area was one for Rs. 2,323 due to the acquisition, conservation and layout of the late Mughal Bagh in the north-east corner of the Qutb enclosure. This garden was previously under private cultivation and its reclamation has permitted of its absorption in the Qutb area, of which it properly forms part. At Tughlaqabad, some needful repair was carried out upon the tomb of Ghyasu-d-Din Tughlaq I, where a great deal of jungle growth was removed from the old walls and a curious little well and water-lift at the rear were repaired. (Conservation.)

Hindu and Buddhist monuments.

Rai Sahib Daya Ram Sahni reports that among the ancient monuments in his Circle, special repairs were carried out during the year under review to (1) the Buddhist remains at Sarnath; (2) the Jaina and Brahmanical monuments at Deogarh in the Jhansi District, and, in the Punjab, to (3) the temple at Malot in Jhelum District, (4) the Baijnath temple at Baijnath, (5) the rock-cut temples at Masrur, (6) the Kangra Fort, and (7) at Taxila, in the Rawalpindi District. The total expenditure on the conservation of Hindu and Buddhist Monuments in the United Provinces amounted to Rs. 5,488-2-5, of which Rs. 998 was defrayed by the Local Government, while the balance of Rs. 4,490-2-5 was provided by an Imperial grant-in-aid from the Director General of Archæology. The cost of the special repairs carried out in the Punjab came to Rs. 5,003-0 8, the whole of which was provided by the Local Government.

United Provinces.

"The operations carried out at Sarnath," the Rai Sahib says, "comprised the general clearance of the greater part of the site, together with arrangements for drainage and certain urgent structural repairs. In connection with these works I had the invaluable advantage of discussing the subject beforehand with Sir John Marshall, who was good enough to inspect the site in December last, and to give me detailed instructions on the spot. The work was carried out under my personal supervision, and it is gratifying to state that considerable progress was made, as the whole of the site, (with the exception of the area between the monasteries and the lake on the north side), was dug up to a depth of one foot, or a foot and a half, completely freed from brickbats, and other rubbish, and then levelled and thoroughly rammed down with stone rollers specially made for the purpose. The slopes of the trenches were improved, and three new flights of steps were provided, at suitable places, for the convenience of visitors. It is intended to cover with turf the whole area thus cleared, but as the time was not suitable for planting grass, the work had to be postponed till the next year. Another important measure that is urgently required is the construction of canals, with bridges at suitable points, for the carrying away of water from the site. Plans and estimates for one such canal, starting from the eastern approach of the Main Shrine and discharging into the *jhil* to the north of the site, were submitted to and approved by the Director General of Archæology in India; but time could not be found to take this work in hand.

"It should be observed that when the area to the south of the Jagat Singh Stupa was being cleared, the remains of a new monastery of the late mediæval period came to light immediately to the west of Kittoe's monastery. It is built on the usual plan with a well-preserved brick well in one corner of the central courtyard. All the cells, with the exception of two, have disappeared; but the operations revealed

(Conservation.) the fact that underneath this building was an earlier monastery of about the same size. The well was cleared down to the water-level and its parapet repaired.

"Since its excavation in 1851-52 by Major M. Kittoe the building known as Kittoe's monastery had received no attention of any kind, with the result that its plan had become so utterly obscure that it was scarcely recognizable as a monastery. In the rains the building becomes one large pool of water, and suitable means for its drainage will have to be devised. The measures carried out during the past year have brought back to view the greater part of the foundations of the building, and throw useful light on the arrangement and history of the monument. In the first place it is found that the central cell in the north row is not, as was imagined by General Cunningham, the chapel of the monastery but the entrance chamber; the rooms that project towards the north being respectively the portico and the guard rooms. Secondly, it seems probable that a second court lies buried to the east side. Lastly, it becomes evident that whereas the monastery excavated by Major Kittoe was presumably constructed in the mediæval period, it is built upon the ruins of an older monastery which, on the evidence of terra-cotta seals I discovered in one of the cells, cannot be later than about the 8th Century A.D.

"The walls of Kittoe's monastery were repaired, and repairs were also carried out to about fifty other structures, stupas, chaityas, etc., most of which are situated in the area around the Jagat Singh Stupa. Among the group of structures to the north of the Dhamekh Stupa, Nos. 71 to 74 were repaired. It also appears that structures Nos. 76 and 78 in the plan of the excavations are in reality one temple consisting of two shrines with a common ante-chamber.

"The operations carried out at Deogarh during the year under report were planned in accordance with the recommendations of Mr. Hargreaves contained in his excellent Inspection and Conservation Notes. I was present at Deogarh throughout these operations. The conservation of the Jaina temples in the Fort was carried out by the Public Works Department, while the excavations at the Gupta and Varāha temples were conducted through the agency of my own office. At the Gupta temple the whole of the basement has been found in a fairly good state of preservation. The upper plinth, however, has entirely disappeared, and the lower plinth has also lost two or three courses at the top. There is a flight of steps on each side of the temple and excavations revealed remains of smaller shrines at the corners of the basement. The sculptures discovered in the diggings included a large number of reliefs showing domestic scenes, many fragments of images of Vishnu, and a well-preserved relief representing the visit of Rāma and Lakshmaṇa to the hermitage of Śabarī (Plate I, *a*). The temple was most probably dedicated to Vishṇu, but I did not find any evidence for its dedication to the ten incarnations as was proposed by Mr. P. C. Mukherji.

"The excavation around the temple was extended for some distance on all sides and disclosed the remains of several smaller shrines, but no surrounding wall or peristyle. The modern stone wall built by the Public Works Department which overlapped three of the stairs of the temple was dismantled, and a new wall will be built next year to keep away cattle, etc.

a. No. 2283. Gupta temple. Panel representing Rama and Lakshman's visit to the hermitage of Sabri. (?)

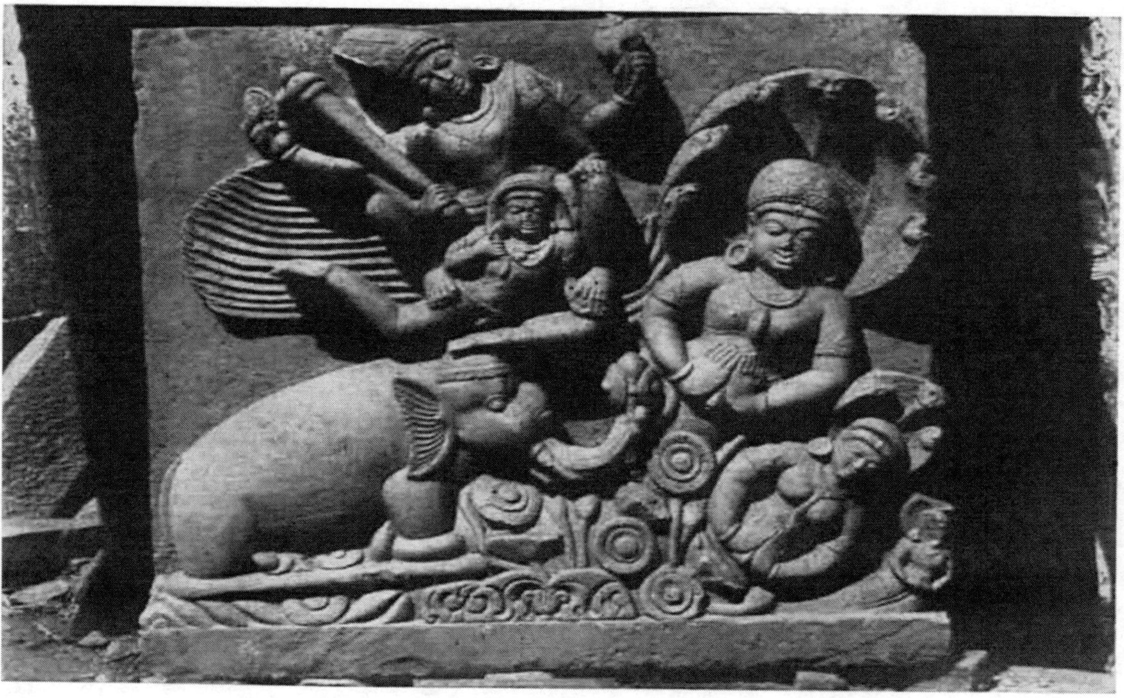

b. No. 2271. Deogarh Fort: Varaha temple. Panel representing the deliverance of the Lord of elephants by Vishnu.

a. No. 2205. Deogarh Fort; general view of Jaina temples Nos. 3 to 9 from N.-E. After clearance of jungle.

b. No. 2260. Deogarh Fort; Jaina temple No. 19. Image of Jaina *yakshi* Chakresvari.

c. No. 2261. Deogarh Fort; Jaina temple No. 19. Image of Jaina *yakshi* Malini or Sumalini.

(Conservation.)

"The Varāha temple mound in the south-west corner of the Deogarh Fort was completely excavated. The portions of the temple that have survived are the greater part of the basement (which must have been rebuilt twice), and the foundations of the shrine. There is no means of ascertaining the exact date of the destruction of the building, but two Nāgarī inscriptions of Samvat 1550 which came to light on the walls of the cella clearly show that the temple must have been in use until that date. One panel representing *śesha-śāyī* Vishnu was visible above the mound at the time of excavation. It is interesting to observe that two other panels exhibiting the deliverance of the lord of elephants by Vishnu (Plate I, *b*), and the penance of Nara and Nārāyaṇa on the Himalayas, were recovered during the excavations. The fact that similar sculptures are inserted in the walls of the Gupta temple lends corroboration to Mr. Hargreaves's suggestion that the temple was an imitation of the Gupta temple. The retaining walls were partially repaired, and the ground around the temple was freed from jungle and débris on all sides.

"The expenditure incurred on the conservation of the Jaina temples, which are 31 in number, was devoted chiefly to the clearance of vegetation from the temples and their surroundings, the thinning of trees and the strengthening of the roofs (Plate II, *a*). The operation revealed the existence of innumerable Jaina images. Those whose connection with the different temples was definitely known were replaced in their temples, while the others were neatly stacked in suitable places. I am of opinion that a suitable shed should be erected in the open space to the west of temple No. 12 for the protection of these images. The clearance around temple No. 12 disclosed the existence of images of the Jaina Yakshinis, with their names engraved on them, on the pillars which support the colonnade around the temple. Other inscribed images of some of the goddesses were also found in the clearance. Four of these belong to temple No. 19. They are Chakreśvarī (Plate II, *b*), Jvālāmālinī (Plate II, *c*), Sarasvatī and Padmāvatīdevī. These sculptures throw useful light on Jaina mythology and art. The Hathi Gate of the Fort also received suitable attention."

Punjab.

In the Punjab Rai Sahib Daya Ram Sahni says that—

"Preliminary operations were carried out at the Malot temple. The ugly modern platform which had been built some years ago was dismantled, and it is gratifying to note that parts of the old basement of the temple have been found intact so that it will be possible to rebuild it on the original plan. A scaffolding has been put up for the proper examination of the roof, and an estimate for further repairs will be prepared after an inspection of the monument. At the Baijnath temple lime-plaster was scraped off the stone carvings, and other minor repairs were carried out. The conservation work carried out at the Kangra Fort consisted of repairs to the arch of the main gateway and the walls adjoining it, and the construction of a dry stone paved path from the main gateway of the Fort to the temple inside it, and of a stone pavement in front of the main gateway. The repairs effected at the rock-cut temples at Masrur embraced the underpinning of masonry, grouting of cracks in the structures, fitting the Hanuman image on the floor, construction of a new *tulasi*-stand,

(Conservation.) clearance of vegetation, excavation around the plinth of the temple and stacking of images."

Taxila. At Taxila the past field season was mainly devoted to conserving the monuments unearthed by Sir John Marshall in previous years, such excavations as were done being limited to the further clearance of these remains. The Director General informs me that on the site of the Dharmarajika Stupa dilapidations in the semi-ashlar facing of the main structure were made good (Plate III *a*), and, for the sake of its stability, the plinth of this stupa had to be repaired, missing Corinthian capitals, pillars and cornices being replaced by new members merely blocked out in the rough without any pretence of restoration. Smaller stupas and sanctuaries surrounding the main edifice were thoroughly overhauled and strengthened. To the west of the site the clearance of the area between the monastery and building G resulted in the discovery of a number of broken Gandhara sculptures (Plate IV, *b*), copper coins and metal objects; while on the north the removal of further débris from the chapels alongside the monastery enclave brought to light some further remains of an earlier period including a small well-preserved relief of Buddha in the *dhyāna-mudrā*, which was still *in situ*, adorning one of the outer walls of the monastery. At the same time considerable progress was also made in the task of levelling and draining the whole site, laying down turf, planting and tidying up the surroundings.

Sir John Marshall also writes that—

" In the upper city of Sirkap an approach was cleared up to the Kunāla monastery by excavating about 700 feet of the inner side of the eastern city wall which here runs up to the hill-side of Hathial, and thus laying bare another interesting feature in this quarter of the site: the repair of the stupa of Kunāla itself was practically brought to a finish; and, in the monastery adjoining, the courtyard and verandah as well as some of the monks' cells were freed from débris. The ground plan of this monastery is similar to that of the monasteries at Jaulian and Mohra Moradu, the masonry used in its construction being of the semi-ashlar variety. In the lower city of Sirkap block A′, B′, C′, D′, E′ and F′ were further excavated and extensively conserved. All their walls were strengthened and rendered water-proof, their open courtyards were turfed over and the interior chambers provided with drains, their surface dressed and sown broad-cast with flowers.

" The conservation measures carried out in the monasteries at Jaulian comprised the repair of the majority of small stupas in the two courtyards, the backing and edging of their stucco reliefs, which, when first unearthed (Plate III, *b*, Plate IV *c* and Plate V, *a* and *b*) were for the most part in a very delicate and fragile state, the repair and water proofing of the walls and floors of chapels, the laying of drains, and the construction of a path-way through the gorge behind the Jaulian hill to connect the Jaulian and Mohra Moradu sites. For the better protection of this site at Jaulian a hut was also erected for the chaukidar on the summit of the hill, and, with a view to lessening some of the difficulties with which work in this part of ancient Taxila has hitherto been carried on, accommodation was provided near the village of Nikra for my assistant, Mr. V. Natesa Aiyar, as well as for the

a. THE DHARMARAJIKA STUPA. GENERAL VIEW FROM N.-E.

b. JAULIAN: STUPA D 4. VIEW FROM S.-E.

Photo-engraved & printed at the Offices of the Survey of India, Calcutta, 1918

a. Gold and jewelled bracelet from Sirkap.

b. Gandhara stone bracket from the Dharmarajika Stupa.

c. Terracotta and stucco heads from Jaulian.

a. JAULIAN: STUPA A 11. STUCCO FIGURE OF A BODHISATTVA IN *DHYANAMUDRA.*

b. JAULIAN: STUPA A 15. ROW OF BUDDHA FIGURES ON EAST FACE OF BASEMENT.

Photo-engraved & printed at the Offices of the Survey of India, Calcutta, 1921

temporary housing of the antiquities from the sites in the immediate neighbourhood." (Conservation.)

The total amount expended on the conservation of ancient monuments in the Bengal Presidency during the year was Rs. 19,320-2-0. Among the monuments under special repair, the following may be mentioned. Rs. 5,053 in addition to Rs. 5,403 previously spent, were devoted to repairs to the tomb of Khan Jahan Ali near Bagerhat in Khulna District, and to the great mosque known as the Satgumbaz. Khan Jahan Ali, the reputed Pioneer of the Sundarbans, is said to have died in 1459 A.D. His tomb is a severely plain brick structure surmounted by a single dome, with the sarcophagus on a triple terraced platform inside, the lowest bank or tier of which was originally covered with blue and white glazed tiles. The tomb itself is in fairly good condition, but certain repairs to the surrounding walls, and to the roof, dome and cornice of the mosque just west of the tomb were called for. The Satgumbaz is a very large mosque with 70 domes, divided internally into seven vaults. Externally the mosque is quite plain, but the east face shows eleven arched openings, and the corners are reinforced with round towers or minarets of substantial thickness In 1907-08 one half of the roof was repaired, when 28 of the domes with interspaces were made secure. The present estimate aimed at repairing most of the remainder, together with miscellaneous items. Opportunity has not yet offered for an inspection of this work. On the cloisters of the Adina Mosque at Panduah in the Malda District a further sum of Rs. 3,004 was spent in addition to Rs. 3,250 laid out in the previous year, the object of the work being to render the exposed hearting of the cloister walls waterproof by coating the surfaces with a thin coat of stained cement and similarly capping the tops of the walls. A certain amount of underpinning was also included, and where essential for the preservation of the remains, bits of facing were to be restored. But the cloisters as a whole are such a complete ruin that nothing beyond the simplest preservation of the remaining fragments can be attempted. The interesting group of late mediæval temples at Barakar, in the Burdwan District, have also been under repair at the cost of the Maharaja Manindra Chandra Nandi Bahadur of Cossimbazar, the estimate coming to Rs. 1,392. The measures involved were mostly of a petty nature and included levelling and draining the grounds. A further estimate for Rs. 3,000 was taken in hand at the Masjidbari Mosque in Bakerganj District, supposed to have been erected in the middle of the 15th century. The mosque was badly overgrown with jungle. The estimate provided for removing this, for cutting encroaching trees, for clearing away rubbish, and dressing the ground around the building for a certain distance, besides the adjustment of the facing bricks on the east side, the grouting of cracks, with repairs to the dome, etc. It should be added, however, that the facing brickwork was never properly bonded with the rest of the wall, and very little of it now remains in consequence. The estimate for special repairs to the Jatar Deul in the Sundarbans provides for replacing the outer facing of new brickwork in the upper part of the temple (an unsatisfactory repair), and eradicating jungle with the subsequent repair of disturbed masonry. A stone floor and steps are also provided, together with clearing and

Bengal.

(Conservation.) levelling the surrounding ground, and laying out pathways. At Vishnupur in the Bankura District various petty works were carried out on 14 of the temples, at a cost of Rs. 2,024 in addition to Rs. 1,444 already spent. But from recent reports it would seem as though the temples are not even yet in a satisfactory condition, and that further measures of conservation will have to be taken up as soon as the Superintendent can frame another Conservation Note.

Bihar and Orissa. In the Province of Bihar and Orissa only two monuments underwent special repairs in 1917-18, *viz.*, the Black Pagoda at Konārak, and the great tomb of Bakhtiyar Khan at Chainpur (Plate VI, *a*) in the Shahabad District, on the latter of which extensive repairs based on Mr. Blakiston's Conservation Note dated the 30th July 1913 were completed at a total cost of Rs. 13,654. The plaster of the great dome had peeled off in patches and it had been proposed to mend these. It was found on examination, however, that the subjacent concrete was itself loose, cracked, and insecure; and before any repair to the plaster was possible, the whole dome had to be encased with a new casing of concrete, six inches thick. The domes on the clerestory level were similarly treated, but with only 3 inches of concrete, and certain cracks at the junction of the verandah roof were also filled in to prevent leakage. Besides these measures, openings were netted to keep out bats, new drain pipes were fixed, broken plaster on the main parapet above the *chajja* was repaired, and certain new *chajja* stones were provided for the main cornice, which was itself renewed where gone. A new *chajja* was constructed also for the crowning cupola above the dome, and the passage through the main gateway was repaired with 2" stone slabs over 3" concrete. Attention was also given to the tombs themselves, and to the floor of the mausoleum, and the flooring of the outside platform was renewed, while the side walls and the steps of the same were also repaired where necessary. Besides all this, the roof of the gateway was mended, loose stones of the *chhatri* were reset, and the north-west corner of the compound wall was rebuilt where it had fallen. One of the four corner kiosks was past repair, but the other three were seen to, and the damaged *chajja* was made good. The site as a whole was furthermore levelled and cleared, and a shed was erected for the chaukidar. In the case of the Black Pagoda at Konārak, the special repairs to be recorded in this Report are those recommended by Mr. Blakiston in his Conservation Note dated the 11th September 1914. They include clearance of sand from part of the courtyard, renewing stone facing at places where hearting was exposed and consequently in danger, pointing (from above) the joints in the lowermost flight of cornices above the Jagamohan, and rebuilding a certain minor shrine on the south side of the main temple after dismantling it. The Superintendent inspected this work in May, 1918, and has issued an Inspection Note dated the 4th of that month, in which he asks to have some of this work done over again. It is understood that considerations of economy had induced the Department of Public Works to make certain alterations in their arrangements for supervision at this site, which have not proved beneficial to the monuments themselves, nor yet in the interests of true economy. It is believed that this matter has already been corrected, and that henceforth the local control of work here will be as satisfactory

a. BAKHTYAR KHAN'S TOMB AT CHAINPUR, DISTT. SHAHABAD.

b. GENERAL VIEW OF ADIL SHAH AND NADIR SHAH'S TOMBS AT BURHANPUR, DISTT. NIMAR, C. P.

as it has been in the past. This is particularly important since the Honourable Mr. Clayton, Chief Engineer, has called attention to the need of repairs to the crowning amalaka of the Jagamohan, and has made proposals for the arrest of this danger which will involve extensive work requiring very careful supervision. It is hoped also that the Superintendent in the Eastern Circle can do something to overcome the disintegration of the surface of the Jagamohan, particularly on its north side, in consultation with the Archæological Chemist. The decay in question according to Mr. Sana Ullah is largely due to the fact that the rain does not wash this side so effectually as it does the others, with the result that the surface here has become impregnated with sea-salts in the course of time. The remedy is thus a thorough washing and brushing of the entire north side of the structure; but adequate measures for this remain to be devised. (Conservation.)

Central Provinces.

The total expenditure on Conservation in the Central Provinces this year amounted to Rs. 13,432 but only four of the estimates for special repairs came individually to more than a thousand rupees each, and only these works need be described in these pages. One of the monuments in question was, I am glad to say, what is referred to in the publications of this Department as Nadir Shah's tomb, at Burhanpur, in the Nimar District (Plate VI, *b*). The evidence for this assignment of the building is more doubtful than could be desired, but in any case it is clearly one of the royal tombs and one which by its architectural interest alone is well deserving of preservation. It is, however, or was, in a parlous condition. Roughly square in plan, the tomb is built of rubble faced with thin stone slabs, and is surmounted with a lofty dome rising from a high, hexagonal drum. But unfortunately the original construction was faulty, as there was no adequate bond between the facing and the core, and the result has been that large portions of the facing have peeled off and fallen away, together with much of the original *chajja* and long stretches of the ornamental cresting of merlons. Close to this building and on the right of it stands the tomb of Adil Shah. A few years ago this, too, was in almost as dilapidated a condition as the tomb of Nadir Shah; but it has been repaired in recent years, and is now less ruinous so that it was legitimately the turn of Nadir Shah's tomb to come in for renovation at this time. The measures carried out refer themselves primarily to the Conservation Note drawn up by Sir John Marshall so long ago as January 1907 and reiterated by Mr. Blakiston five years later, funds not having been available for the work heretofore. The revised estimate amounts to Rs. 4,506, and was first taken in hand in 1916-17, when a sum of Rs. 1,042 was spent, to which a further expenditure of Rs. 1,947 is to be added this year. Most of the work consists of refacing, but repairs to the platform and to the dome are also provided, including rebuilding the former where necessary. The interior platform with the actual tombs is also to be renovated and in part repaved, but the estimate excludes renewing brackets, *chajja* and cornice and aims only at preserving the ruin from further decay, not at restoration as such. No ornamental carving of new stone work is contemplated, but only the careful blocking in of simple string courses, projections, and the like, to maintain the original contours. In addition to this work, an estimate for Rs. 3,569 has been taken in hand at Asir-

(Conservation.) garh, in the same District, for special repairs to the Jami Masjid in the fort. An inscription in a neighbouring tank shows that this mosque, which is a small replica of the great mosque at Burhanpur, was built in the period of Shah Jahan. It is excellently finished, with a court surrounded by cloisters. During the British occupation of the fortress, however, this building was used as a barrack, and various accretions had come into being, such as a reading-room located on the roof, etc.; certain windows had been cut and certain arches blocked up, so that all in all the place had been considerably transformed. The estimate here referred to aims at undoing the damage done by this occupation, and restoring the mosque to its condition prior to this misuse of it. Very little structural repair was needed, most of the work consisting of removing the unsightly accretions mentioned above. But Mr. Blakiston, in his Conservation Note dated the 29th March 1913 (which is the basis for the estimate in question), recommended the renewal of certain *chajja* stones, and this work, with the necessary repair of brackets, is also provided for. The whitewash covering the stone columns inside is also to be removed, and the surroundings to be tidied up generally. Another monument to which much needed repairs have been effected this season is the graceful and ornate temple at Gondai in the Drug District. The temple consists of a fairly slender, tapering śikhara, with a shallow porch on the south or front side. The cella is distinguished externally from the tower proper by a horizontal banding of the former contrasting with vertical banding in the latter. The whole is built of sandstone, and differs from most temples of this general class by having the background as a rule covered with a delicate sculptured ornament in low relief, while the main statuary is boldly advanced and thus given the proper emphasis,—a point in which the Gondai temple reminds one somewhat of the Rājarāni temple at Bhuvanesvara, where similar good taste is revealed. Mr. Blakiston dates the shrine tentatively in the late 15th or early 16th century, but no basis for accurate dating is known. But the absence of mortar in the joints as well as the æsthetic quality of the decoration, would of themselves seem to suggest a somewhat earlier date than even the 15th century. From a distance the monument would have seemed to be in good condition, even before the present repairs were taken in hand, but closer inspection would have disclosed the fact that the temple as a whole had a bad list to south, and that many of the foundation stones had been thrust out of position or been crushed to such an extent that underpinning and like measures were no longer adequate to preserve it. After consultation with Sir John Marshall it was decided that the whole superstructure would have to be completely dismantled, and then re-erected again precisely as before, after adequate foundations had been laid. In his Conservation Note, dated the 12th August 1914, Mr. Blakiston gave minute and explicit instructions for this work, and the estimate now reported to have been completed, with a further expenditure this season of Rs. 6,625, covered the measures he advised. At Balapur, in Akola District, the strongly but simply built fort consisting of a pentagonal enclosure with five large bastions built all within a many-sided fort with 11 bastions also came in for special repairs this year. An inscription on the outer gate says that the fort was built in 1757 by

a. VITTALA TEMPLE AT HAMPI: S GATEWAY, SHOWING ENTRANCE BLOCKED WITH LARGE PILLARS TO SUPPORT THE BROKEN LINTELS AND ROOF SLABS.

b. THE SAME: SHOWING PILLARS IN THE ENTRANCE REMOVED AND IRON GIRDERS FIXED IN PLACE OF SAME.

Photo-engraved & printed at the Offices of the Survey of India, Calcutta, 1916

Ismail Khan, first Nawab of Ellichpur. It is one of the strongest forts in Berar and is picturesquely situated at the junction of the rivers Man and Mhais. In 1917-18 a sum of Rs. 726 was spent, in addition to Rs. 560 previously laid out, covering Mr. Blakiston's Conservation Note dated the 13th February, 1913. The retaining wall around the battlements on the east (wrongly printed "south" in the Note) of the inner fort was bulging, necessitating buttressing, and a crack in the large well within the inner fort was strengthened, in addition to various other repairs here and there, too petty to require specific mention. (Conservation).

Southern Circle.

In the Southern Circle, the total expenditure on all classes of Conservation comes this year to Rs. 22,625-11-11, distributed over 115 items, some of them of course petty, and only two running to more than a thousand rupees. This is, though, to a certain extent misleading, for at Hampi seventeen different works were taken in hand, seven at Tanjore, six at Penukonda, and so on, so that really more extensive work was done at individual sites than the large number of single estimates would at first seem to imply. At Hampi the work on the Vittala temple consisted of pointing up the open joints of various portions, flooring inside the mandapa, certain underpinning, constructing buttress walls for part of the north mandapa, and the insertion of rolled steel beams to support broken lintels (Plate VII). Near the Talarigatta Gate the fallen portion of the fort wall was re-packed, and the Vishnu temple to the west of Soolai Bazaar was tidied up generally, a work which included the removal of mounds of accumulated earth from the interior. Similar clearance was effected at the Jain temple on the Hemakutam Rock, and the Ganigatta Jain temple, as well as to the Vishnu temple No. 3. At the Underground Temple Mr. Longhurst says that the fallen cutstone walls were rebuilt, and sundry other repairs, to drains, etc., were carried out. The largest single work at Hampi however aimed at preserving the palace buildings, where the expenditure comes to Rs. 1,823. At Tanjore three special repair works were taken in hand. Two worn out pillars were replaced in the Maharaja Sabha in the Palace; some new plastering was done to the front tower of the big temple, and in the Jerathkhana the mud walls which had been erected between the arches were removed so as to let in more light and air. The special repairs at the old Fort at Arcot were brought to completion this season with a further expenditure of Rs. 791, and the clearance of vegetation from the fort walls at Wandiwash was also taken in hand, but the work was not completed in the year under report. The largest single estimate dealt with during this season was one for Rs. 3,252 for sundry repairs to the fort and other monuments at Gingee, in the South Arcot District, where improvements to a considerable list of ancient monuments are being carried out, and the work is still incomplete. The fallen portion of the rampart to the fort at Bekal in the South Kanara District was rebuilt and the whole cleared of vegetation, and similar improvements were effected to the Hill Fort at Hosdrug and the Sultan's Battery near Mangalore, the works at both places consisting largely of jungle clearance with various minor repairs. Further special repairs costing Rs. 755 were carried out to the Buddhist chaityas, stupas and rock-cut caves at Guntapalle in the Ellore Taluk of the Kistna District and others to the remains

(Conservation.) of a Buddhist stupa on the hill at Jaggayyapeta. The Asoka inscriptions on the hill at Jaugada, in Ganjam District, were fenced around, and petty repairs were effected to the remains at Amaravati. But the thorough conservation of this latter site is still outstanding. It is hoped that before long some scheme can be devised for putting this once important site into a more satisfactory condition than its present one.

Frontier Circle. The only work of conservation undertaken in the Frontier Circle during the year was at Taxila, (a portion of which site falls within the limits of the Hazara District), and aimed at the preservation of the stupas and monasteries brought to light at Jaulian (see Plates III, IV and V). For this work an Imperial grant-in-aid amounting to Rs. 5,500 was utilized, while a further grant of Rs. 3,600 was applied to the erection of a godown for the temporary accommodation of the antiquities from this and neighbouring sites, and to the other works mentioned on pp. 8 and 9 above. Pandit Natesa Aiyar reports that shortage of funds and shortage of officers in the Engineering Department combined to prevent further repairs being taken in hand at places like Takht-i-Bahi and Jamalgarhi, although he adds that these sites stand in need of early attention. That being the case, it is hoped that some means will be found of overcoming the difficulties, for the importance of these ancient Frontier monuments is such as to render their conservation a matter of imperative necessity.

Burma. During the year under report a sum of Rs. 11,188 was spent on the maintenance and repair of ancient monuments in Burma. No grant-in-aid was received, and the entire cost of these works was consequently borne by the Local Government. Out of the total, a sum of Rs. 541 was spent on special repairs to Pagodas in the Kyaukse District and to the remains of the East India Company's Factory at Hainggyi. Mr. Taw Sein Ko reports that these works were of a minor nature, and consisted chiefly in clearing away jungle from around the Pagodas, and providing them with entrance gates, while the remains at Hainggyi were enclosed with a fence. It had been intended to erect a memorial brass tablet on the walls of the Factory, setting forth its history; but the cost involved was found to be so excessive in present conditions that the project had to be postponed. The monuments in question were selected for conservation more for their historical value than for their architectural merit. The Pagodas in the Kyaukse District—the Shwezigon Pagoda, the Nandawye Pagoda, the Letthe Pagoda and the Chanthaya Pagoda—constitute landmarks in the history of Burma. They were constructed to commemorate the events near the close of the 13th century A.D. when the three Shan brothers Athinkaya, Yazathingyan and Thihathu established themselves at Myinzaing, Metkaya and Pinle respectively, after the subversion of the Pagan monarchy by the Chinese in 1287 A.D. These monuments thus indicate the eclipse of Pagan as the seat of Burmese power and the transfer of Burmese sovereignty from the Burmans to the Shans, who established themselves on the upper reaches of the Irrawaddy and laid the foundations of Ava as a rival of Pagan in art, refinement, and culture. The remains of the East India Company's Factory at Hainggyi, on the other hand, form a silent witness of early British enterprise, and of the efforts made for British commercial and political expansion in Burma. The Factory was established in 1753, but was abandoned a few years later, in 1759, when the officers and men of the garrison stationed there, being suspected of treachery and of helping the Talaings with arms and ammunition, met with a tragic end at the hands of the infuriated soldiery of Alaungpaya. Unhappily the remains now consist merely of brick walls in a dilapidated condition. **(Conservation.)**

An important incident in the year's work in Burma was the visit of inspection paid by Sir John Marshall in the months of December and January. After visiting the Shwedagon and Sule Pagodas at Rangoon, the Director General proceeded to Mandalay, where, during a fortnight's halt, the many monuments at this centre were inspected, and measures for the preservation of the palace buildings in particular were considered with the local authorities. On the 12th January Pagan was reached, and the next few days were devoted to an examination of the monuments and a consideration of the problems at this extensive and important centre.

At Mandalay and even at Pagan despite the admirable work already achieved at the latter place, long lists of conservation works are still outstanding, some of which are of a decidedly urgent nature, but obviously not much can be done until financial conditions improve. What is most essential at the former site is the formulating of a definite policy and the drawing up of a definite scheme or programme of conservation. Along both these lines substantial progress has been made in the year under review, thanks to the long and detailed Notes on this subject drawn up by Sir John Marshall and also by His Honour Sir Reginald Craddock, in which the needs and even the future policy of the Local Government find clear and encouraging statement. With the Government so sympathetic as His Honour's Note shows them to be, the future of conservation in Burma should be assured, and so soon as peace is restored, it is anticipated that a systematic campaign can be taken in hand. Even before that time, however, preliminary steps are to be taken toward the repair of those portions of the Mandalay palace which are in most urgent need of attention, and to this end a substantial grant-in-aid from Imperial sources is proposed for Burma in the coming year. Where present neglect would only lead to greatly increased expenditure later, it is manifestly unwise to postpone the work.

On this principle it is satisfactory to note that even under the stress of the war, Mr. Taw Sein Ko reports that the Buddhist community in Burma are showing the opposite of parsimony in undertaking repairs to some of their notable monuments. Thus the people of the Pegu District, Mr. Taw Sein Ko tells me, have decided on repairs to the Shwehmawdaw Pagoda at an approximate cost of four or five lakhs of rupees. The *hti*, the *amlaka* and the concentric rings below the *amlaka* of this Pagoda, measuring all in all more than one hundred feet in height, were thrown down by a severe shock of earthquake on the 5th July 1917. That certain differences of opinion arose as to the best course to follow in these circumstances, and that considerable intensity of feeling existed locally, is well shown by Mr. Taw Sein Ko's interesting account of these proceedings in his Provincial Report for this year. But happily the matter was at length settled amicably and

(Conservation.) unanimously, and the Pagoda Trustees have now decided to rebuild the damaged portion in reinforced concrete, with the help of the local officer of the Public Works Department, and it is hoped that the work wil lbe completed three years hence. Without expressing any opinion as to the propriety of the particular measures adopted, this Department would like to record its appreciation of the very admirable spirit shown by the Buddhists in this matter, a spirit which, admirable at any time, is beyond praise in the conditions which obtain.

Western Circle. At Champanir the Jami Masjid, the Godhra Gateway, the Mandvi or the six-domed entrance to the palace and the Bohra-ki-Masjid were made water-tight. In the Lila Gumbaz the old ashlar masonry of the rear and south walls was dismantled and reset and new ashlar facing was supplied to fill gaps. The buttresses at the back were also dismantled and rebuilt as they had separated from the main wall and got out of plumb. The ashlar masonry on the outside of the eastern wall was repaired and reset. The brick walls on the north and south of the Mandvi were strengthened and the ashlar facing of the east side dismantled and rebuilt. Some broken and missing slabs of the roof were renewed. Owing to excessive rainfall the back wall of the Kevda Masjid collapsed. Arrangements were made to rebuild and strengthen this wall, before the beginning of the monsoon, and to carry on the work throughout the year. The total expenditure on Special Repairs to the monuments at Champanir was Rs. 8,809.

In the Ibrahim Roza at Bijapur, four new support arches were begun under the inner arcade and were very nearly finished. The openings which lead to the real tomb were closed with expanded metal in wooden frames. All vertical and horizontal cracks in the dome of the Gol-Gumbaz were filled with specially prepared lime after excavating the cracks to a depth of six inches. Some mischievous person or persons have chipped off portions of the great gun called the Malik-i-Maidan. As the matter was brought to the notice of the Government the Executive Engineer took steps to prevent a recurrence of such mischievousness, and had the fallen battlements on the eastern side rebuilt, and the walls of the gun bastion reconstructed. A doorway in the wall is now the only entrance to the top of the bastion.

All modern infillings were removed from the openings in the façade of the Jami Masjid. The marble steps of the open-air pulpit in front of the main arcade were dismantled and reset. A compound wall was begun around the Jod Gumbaz and the compound partly cleared of its ancient accumulation of cactus shrubs. The Special Repairs to Jahan Begum's Mahal at Ainapur were begun, but work had to be stopped as water percolated into the pits dug for laying the foundations of buttresses. Iron grills were provided in the openings on the outside. The land and the houses situated between the masjid and the tomb of Jahan Begum were acquired. The roof ot the Jain temple in the Mission compound at Pattadkal was repaired. At Badami special repairs to the following monuments have been completed :—

(1) Small temple on the knoll close to the upper temple.

(2) Temple on the spur to the south-east of the Gurali Temple.

The repairs to the following monuments are in progress:— (Conservation.)

(1) Bhutnath Temples to the north of Badami Tank, Group 1.

(2) Bhutnath Temples to east of Badami Tank.

(3) The Banasankari Tank.

In the Dharwar District temporary buttresses were provided, deformed stone facing was reset and new ashlar masonry was provided to fill gaps in the Ramesvara Temple at Balambid. The repairs to the temple of Someswar at Haralhalli are in progress. Here some broken slabs were removed and an accumulation of earth was dug away from the roof. In the temple of Manikeśvara at Lakkundi near Gadag, certain walls were underpinned, partly dismantled and rebuilt. In the North Kanara District, *chhajja* slabs and plinth slabs were reset in the temple of Śiva at Somasāgar. Initial repairs are in progress on the temple of Siva at Sonda in the same district. In the Ahmadabad District the repairs to the principal tomb at Vatwa were completed and those to Raju-ki-Roza were in progress. The cracks in the dome of the Khan Masjid at Dholka were filled up. In the Kaira District the work of rebuilding the Śikhara of the temple of Galateśvara at Sarnal is half-finished and will be completed in 1918-19. A new wall was built on the top of cave No. 35 at Kanheri in the Thana District. The numbering of the caves was renewed at the same place. In the Nasik District a frame of channel iron was fixed in the south porch of the temple of Mahādeva at Ambegaon. At the same place angle irons were fixed diagonally across each column and a wire fence erected.

Rajputana. At Ajmer the special repairs to the Arhai-din-ki-jhopra were completed. The restorations to the temples at Dilwara are in progress. Pointing has again unfortunately been done on the carved surface of the interior by the Manager of the temple.

Central India. At Mandu the south side of the balcony of the Jami Masjid was conserved and the compound wall on this side was finished. Whitewash was removed from the wall and the platform in front of the mimbar. The restoration of broken lintels in the tomb of Hoshang Shah could not be taken in hand as marble slabs of the size required could not be procured.

The expenditure by the Dhar State of Rs. 4,046, in addition to that on the conservation of monuments, in maintaining roads leading to the principal remains at Mandu, deserves special mention.

Kashmir. Pandit Hirananda Shastri, Archæological Superintendent in Kashmir, reports that conservation has been carried out this year at eight different monuments, at a total cost of Rs. 6,691-5-1 against a budget provision of Rs. 7,000, in addition to a sum of Rs. 2,950 laid out on repairs to the old palace at Leh in Ladakh, through the agency of the Public Works Department. At Avantipur the work consisted of clearing away débris from the south and west sides of the temple around which a space of some 23 feet has now been left, the earth being banked back from this path with a slope of 1 in 1. The slope cut at the south has been turfed like the one in front of the sanctuary, and besides this a culvert has been constructed at the south-east corner to drain off rain-water. At Pandrethan, as is well known, the Siva shrine has long stood in the midst of water. The drain cut previously with a view to drawing off this water was deepened this year to

(Conservation.) allow of an increased flow, and to expose the basement and the floor of the temple, hitherto flooded; and an endeavour was also made to locate and examine the various small springs which are responsible for this accumulation. As regards the Shankaracharya temple on the Takht-i-Suleman above Srinagar, materials were collected so as to permit of starting in the spring of next year the repairs recommended by Sir John Marshall. At Pattan the area round the temple which was occupied by the courtyard and the peristyle has been properly dressed and turfed according to the plan of the structure, so as to give an idea of what it was originally; and the miniature temple standing in a spring opposite the dak-bungalow has been reconstructed by order of the Durbar, together with its tanks and stone pavement. Pukka steps and outlets have been provided, and the ground outside has been levelled and tidied up. The so-called Dhathamandir, "a ruinous temple," midway between Uri and Rampur, and sometimes known as the Bandi temple, also came in for special attention. The Superintendent visited this monument in company with Sir John Marshall, and subsequently, while reserving the conservation of the main building for next year, removed a considerable amount of débris on the east and west, and in place of the ruinous and untidy stone fence erected a wooden one all around the site, as preliminary to carrying out the suggestions made by the Director General. Work was also begun on a culvert at the north-west corner, and on a retaining wall a little above the foot of the hill on the south side, to ensure the safety of the sanctuary. In addition to these measures, petty improvements were effected at both the Nishat and the Shalamar Gardens, at the former of which parts of the surrounding wall were repaired and the two *Baradaris* on the cross channels opposite the marble pavilion were re-roofed.

H. E. H. the Nizam's dominions.

In the Hyderabad State activity continues to centre mainly in the Aurangabad district. Repairs to the Buddhist caves at the town itself and the Śaivite temple at Anwa were completed at a combined cost of Rs. 7,861. At Ellora the operations are in progress, Rs. 8,357 having been spent during the year out of the first sanctioned estimate for Rs. 30,019. A second estimate for Rs. 40,000 is before the Finance Department for sanction. The preservation of the Ajanta caves also has been taken in hand and caves I, II, VI, X, XII, XV and XVI are under repair. His Exalted Highness's Government have asked Sir John Marshall to engage on their behalf the services of an Italian expert for a cold season to execute suitable repairs to the frescoes, the protection of which has been a matter of anxious consideration to His Exalted Highness's Government.

His Exalted Highness's Government have also sanctioned a sum of B. G. Rs. 5,000 for the French savant, Monsieur Foucher, to write a monograph on the iconography of the Ajanta paintings. The monograph will be illustrated by the three-colour process: the Director General of Archæology is arranging with a well-known firm in England about the production of the plates.

During the year Mr. Yazdani inspected the Jami mosque at Biloli in the Nandod district and suggested suitable measures for its conservation. The mosque was built by one Sarfraz Khan in 1027 A. H. during the reign of Muhammad Quṭb Shah. The style of architecture is rather poor in effect. The arched

a. JAMI MASJID, BILOLI (NANDED).

b. TOLI MASJID, COLONNADE, FRONT VIEW.

Photo-engraved & printed at the Offices of the Survey of India, Calcutta, 19[illegible]

AUNDHA TEMPLE, SIKARA (UPPER PORTION IS MODERN).

Photo-engraved & printed at the Offices of the Survey of India, Calcutta, 1910

a. Naganatha temple, Aundha, from South West (Western half).

b. Dichpalli Temple, Ellora.

Photo-engraved & printed at the Offices of the Survey of India, Calcutta, [illegible]

openings of the hall are somewhat squat in the style of early Muslim buildings, (Conservation.) while the minarets are extremely slender, mere toy articles and evidently never meant for use (Plate VIII, *a*). Another Quṭb Ṡhahi monument, the conservation of which the Superintendent has recommended to His Exalted Highness's Government, is the Toli Masjid in the suburbs of Hyderabad on the way to Golconda (Plate VIII, *b*). It was built by Musa Khan, a dignitary of the Court of 'Abdullah Quṭb Shah, who held the office of Mahalldar (Lord Chamberlain) but in the time of war he played the rôle of general as well. An inscription carved in the prayer niche gives 1082 A.H. (1671 A.D.) as the date of the erection of the building. The mosque is situated within an extensive enclosure which originally had a large garden but no vestige of it remains now. The prayer chamber consists of a double hall, the outer apartment having five arched openings and the inner only three, the place of the extreme openings towards north and south being occupied by two niches built in the pillar and lintel style. In the inner hall, at the western end, there is a prayer niche in the form of a semi-decagon. Two lofty minarets flank the building at each side and a number of small cupolas adorn the roof. The lower part of the mosque up to the roof is built of ashlar masonry while the upper part is constructed of brick and lime so as to carry decorations in stucco. The chief feature of the building is its decorations, which exhibit a strong Hindu influence in motif as well as in sentiment. To wit, the circular earthen pot, which is so common a theme in Hindu architectural ornamentation, is largely adopted here—the shaft of the minarets rise from pot-shaped bases, and the façade is adorned with rows of black basalt pots cut in relief. Again, elephant tusk brackets, which are absolutely Hindu in origin—the figure of an animal being repugnant to orthodox Muslim taste—have been used profusely in the mosque. Further, there are niches in the pillar and lintel style identical in form with niches in temples for the accommodation of images. Another Hindu feature which may escape the notice of a casual visitor is that just as the Hindu adorns the exterior surface of the temple with miniature *sikharas* and other architectural detail, in the mosque also the tops of niches are adorned with miniature mosques and minarets. The Superintendent also examined the beautiful Hindu temple at Aundah (Parbhani district) and Dichpalli (Nizamabad district) (Plates IX and X). The former is a magnificent building most artistically planned and adorned with exquisite carvings. It has a close resemblance to the famous temple at Halebid in architectural design as well as in decoration and if, according to the terminology of Mysore scholars, we call this style Hoysala, the designation would appear absurd in the case of the Parbhani temple because it was not built by the rulers of that dynasty. If the name "Chalukyan" given by Fergusson to this style is not considered to be appropriate, the only other adequate term would seem to be "Dekhani."

The temple at Dichpalli is another fine example of this style. The Superintendent immediately after his examination of the building in December 1917, proposed effective measures for its conservation, and they have since been approved by His Exalted Highness's Government and the work will be started shortly.

(Conservation.) Gwalior.

Owing to paucity of funds little conservation was possible in Gwalior State. The only monument where special repairs were undertaken was the tomb known as the Gumbazka Maqbara at Bhilsa (Plate XI). Petty repairs to the walls of the Survaya Fort and to the Museum shed at Besnagar were also executed.

Ancient Monuments Act.

In the Bombay Presidency agreements were entered into with the owners of 15 monuments. 34 out of the 35 monuments in the United Provinces referred to in the last year's report have been declared protected and in addition 8 others. In the Punjab four monuments have been protected, 13 in the Province of Delhi and in the Southern Circle seven. The notice of protection has been withdrawn in the case of one monument in the latter circle. Difficulty has been experienced in persuading certain owners of ancient monuments in Bijapur town to enter into agreements with the Government.

Listing of ancient monuments.

The photographic survey of the Ancient Monuments in the Province of Bihar and Orissa was continued during the year. The two photographers attached to the Superintendent's office for this purpose visited places in the Shahabad, Monghyr, and Hazaribagh Districts. In the Eastern Circle the revision of the list is now principally in the hands of the Assistant Superintendent, who, it is hoped, will be able to bring to a conclusion the list of Monuments in the Tirhut Division without delay. In the Frontier Circle a hundred monuments in the Peshawar District were examined and listed. Progress in the listing of ancient remains in Burma was somewhat handicapped owing to the absence on deputation of the Assistant Superintendent.

Delhi.

In the province of Delhi the preliminary list of monuments in the Delhi Zail was passed for printing. The list for the Mehrauli Zail was finished and the Badarpur Zail was taken in hand. It is proposed to publish this last list when ready along with the list for the Mahrauli Zail as Vol. III of its Series.

Gwalior.

The listing of ancient monuments was also continued in the Gwalior State by Mr. M. B. Garde, the State Archæological Officer. He visited thirty-three villages in the Ujjain, Shajapore, Mandsaur, Easagarh and Narwar Districts and listed 166 Monuments. Besides these he revisited some 50 monuments in the Bhilsa and Mandsaur Districts and took photographs, which he had been unable to take last year. The monuments listed comprise rock-cut caves, images, temples, inscriptions, memorial pillars, forts, palaces, mosques, tombs and other miscellaneous antiquities. He discovered several interesting monuments, among them being a number of rock-cut caves at Khijaira Bhop in the Mandesaur District, which he describes as being probably of the 8th or 9th century A.D. Some monolithic columns in the vicinity of the ancient town of Mandsaur are worthy of note. Dr. Fleet has described them in detail in his "Gupta inscriptions" p. 143. The columns now are lying broken and appear to deserve attention, having been erected by King Yashodhharman in the first half of the 6th century A.D. as evidenced by an inscription.

Rajputana.

The task of listing the ancient remains of Rajputana was started in 1904 by Mr. D. R. Bhandarkar and in the six succeeding years lists were prepared by him of the monuments in the States of Sirohi, Marwar, Jodhpur, Udaipur, Jaipur, and Kishengarh. Since 1912 however, owing to other and more important

GHUMBAZ KA MAQBARA AT BHILSA (GWALIOR STATE): BEFORE CONSERVATION.

GHUMBAZ KA MAQBARA AT BHILSA (GWALIOR STATE): IN COURSE OF CONSERVATION.

Photo-engraved & printed at the Offices of the Survey of India, Calcutta, 1916

tasks in other parts of the Western Circle, the only further progress made has been in the Sirhoi State where a few remains were catalogued by Dr. V. Sukthankar in the winter of 1916-17, and as there seemed little prospect of the work being resumed by the Superintendent or his assistant, Sir John Marshall decided to make use of the services of Dr. Tessitori, who is in charge of the Bardic and Historical Survey of Rajputana. He accordingly took up the archæological exploration of the Bikaner State, in 1916, and has now submitted his first report on the subject. **(Listing of ancient monuments.)**

Dr. Tessitori has made it a point to examine, either personally or through a trustworthy explorer, every bit of the country, village for village, so as to make it practically certain that nothing is left behind. The area he has so far explored represents about a half of the Bikaner territory. The country is not very favourable for archæological exploration, for on the one hand the enormous distances between one village and another make travelling slow and difficult; and on the other owing to the general dearth of stone there are few architectural or sculptural monuments of note and importance. Indeed, outside of the city of Bikaner only one temple of substantial construction has so far been discovered in this tract, *viz.*,—the Jaina temple of Susāṇī at Morkhāṇā [1]—and scattered fragments of two or three others have been found at Palta [2]; apart from these, all the lithic monuments found in the district are *sati*-tablets, *kirtistambhas*, and *chhattris*. *Sati*-tablets are so common in the southern part of the Bikaner State that there is hardly a village without a few of them. But in the northern part of the State they are entirely unknown. The oldest examples were found at Bhādlā and Morkhānā (12th century A.D.), Rāsisar, Kanvalisar (13th—14th century), and Chhāpar (13th century), and these refer to Chhīkana, Sānkhalā, and Mohila Rajputs, respectively. Two or three *sati*-tablets referring to Chiefs of note who played a prominent part in the Rāṭhor colonization of Bikaner at the end of the 15th and the beginning of the 16th century A.D., were found in the tract of the desert to the south of the capital. Though of little value archæologically, the *sati*-tablets are of considerable importance from the point of view of local history and of the history of Rajputana in general. Dr. Tessitori has been able to illustrate the examples found fully and exhaustively. Thanks to the information gained by Dr. Tessitori from local chronicles he has been able to identify the heroes of the majority of these *Sati* memorials and to use the monuments as a means of amplifying his history. Hundreds of *sati*-tablets referring to Pallivāl brahmins and dating from the 16th century onwards, were found in villages to the west of Gajner, but these are of less historical interest. **(Exploration.) Bikaner.**

Dr. Tessitori explains the *sati*-tablet as a monument of the Rajputs *par excellence*, which in Northern Rajputana came into vogue towards the beginning of the 12th century A.D. Before this time, according to him the function of the *sati*-tablets was fulfilled by the *govardhana*. In outward appearance the *govardhana* is identical with the modern *kirtistambha*, being provided with four sculptured faces representing Vishṇu, Sūrya, Siva and Gaṇeśa. The only difference between

---

[1] 22 miles S. E. of Bikaner.
[2] 80 miles N. E. of Bikaner.

(Exploration.) them is that the *kirtistambha* is commemorative whereas the ***govardhana*** is a funerary monument. The funerary character of the ***govardhana*** had been ignored until Dr. Tessitori digging around the shafts of ***govardhanas*** of the 11th century or so at Uderāmsar and Kilchü—two villages a few miles S. and S.E. of Bikaner—exhumed a certain number of earthen pots containing burnt bones and ashes.

Like a true Rajput country, Bikaner possesses quite a number of forts, partly *kachchā* and partly built of brick or of rubble. A large proportion of these, however, are quite small and uninteresting. The most important of all excepting the Bikaner Fort, is the fort of Bhatner (modern Hanumāngadh), which is an imposing structure, entirely built of bricks, enclosing an area of over 1,000 feet square (Plate XII Fig. 1). This fort has had a glorious past, and had a considerable importance even as early as the end of the 14th century A.D. when, according to the Muhammadan chroniclers, it was taken by Timur and razed to the ground (1398 A.D.). Naturally, during its secular history, the fort must have undergone countless repairs. The last of these—chiefly to the eastern wall—were made at the expense of the Bikaner Darbar only about ten years ago.

The comparatively poor results of the exploration with regard to temples and other lithic monuments of plastic and architectural value, have been compensated by the discovery of some very interesting Buddhist remains at Sūratgadh, a small town 113 miles NE of Bikaner, and at Baropal, a village in the neighbourhood. Sūratgadh possesses a fort built by Mahārāja Sūrat Singh of Bikaner about the year 1800 A.D. It is entirely built of bricks, many of them taken from ancient Buddhist structures, these bricks being partly plain and partly decorated with ornamental and architectural designs. The most interesting pieces, which have now been removed to Bikaner, include fragments of cornices, frames, and friezes with acanthus leaf (Plate XII Figs. 2, 3, 4), chequered, and squamellate designs, brackets, rosettes, etc. Three representations of animal figures: a winged crouching Garuḍa (Plate XII Fig. 5); a monster with bovine head, human bust, and a single elephantine foot (Plate XII Fig. 6); and an elephant carrying on his back a man in a prone position (Plate XII Fig. 7), are especially noteworthy. In all these fragments the influence of the Gandhāra school is very apparent. According to the local tradition the brick materials of which the Sūratgadh fort is built, originally came from Rang Mahal, a village about 2 miles NE of the former place. From the same village—which is undoubtedly an ancient site—apparently came three very interesting terracotta panels, which were lying in a small chamber in the Bikaner Fort. These include: a representation of Siva and Pārvatī (Plate XIII Fig. 2), a representation of Krishṇa in the act of uplifting the mount Govardhana (Plate XIII Fig. 1), and a representation of an idyllic scene between a man and a woman standing under a tree (Plate XIII Fig. 3). Ten more terracotta reliefs still more interesting and unique in their way, representing male and female figures from the waist upwards in various attitudes, were recovered from Barapal, a village 7 miles NE of Rang Mahal. "A general and very characteristic feature of all these reliefs," says Dr. Tessitori, "is the classical treatment of the drapery and of the hair, which at once betrays the influence of the Gan-

Fig. 1. HANUMANGARH, BIKANIR.

Fig. 3.

Fig. 4.

Fig. 2.

Fig. 5.

Fig. 6. Fig. 7.

TERRACOTTAS FROM BIKANIR.

Fig. 1.

Fig. 2.

Fig. 3.

Fig. 4.

Fig. 5.

Fig. 6.

Fig. 7.

TERRACOTTAS FROM BIKANIR.

Photo-engraved & printed at the Offices of the Survey of India, Calcutta, [illegible]

dhāra school. The men are represented bare-headed and beardless, with naked busts except for a collar-like ornament round their necks and a sort of narrow scarf thrown over one or both their shoulders (Plate XIII Figs. 4, 5). The females are represented variously, but mostly with naked or half-naked busts, only partially covered by a scarf hanging from their head down the back and gathered up over the arms, and partly Indian and partly classical ornaments (Plate XIII Figs. 6, 7)." The most striking classical feature of these reliefs is perhaps the bodice worn by the women represented in Plate XIII Fig. 7, which with its short sleeves and armour-like decorations, has a very marked Roman appearance. (Exploration.)

Along the dry bed of the Ghagghar in the northern part of the Bikaner State, a large number of *theris* or ancient mounds have been explored, and from the nature of the sherds with which they are littered, Dr. Tessitori has concluded that "they may represent necropolises of the Johiyās, the descendants of the ancient Uaudheyas, who once inhabited and in part still inhabit that region. It appears that bodies were first cremated, and then the few bones left from the pyre were collected in small earthen vases and buried in these mounds. The method of inhumation varied—it probably changed with the times:—in some cases all the cinerary vases are collected in a large urn, which is buried in a perpendicular position; in other cases the vases are spread on the bottom of a square or rectangular ditch and then covered with a layer of large bricks; in other cases they are enshrined in a circular tumulus having a rounded dome and, in one instance, at least, a central relic chamber." From the great height of some of these mounds, and the great number of stratifications contained in them, it would seem that the practice must have extended over at least a thousand years, but whether Dr. Tessitori is right in connecting its origin with the Buddhist custom of relic inhumation and worship, only further investigation can decide.

The buildings in the Panala Fort had not been photographed or thoroughly inspected before Mr. R. D. Banerji's visit in September. The majority of the monuments were built by the officers of the Kings of Bijapur. Among others special mention ought to be made of the following buildings:— Bombay.

The Tin-Darwaza or a series of three gates leading to the valley, one of the largest gateways of the fort. The outer gate still bears marks of British shells of the war of 1840. An inscription on this side records the erection of the gate during the reign of Sultan Ibrahim Adil Shah I in 1547 A.D. The interior of the Tin-Darwaza contains a number of guard rooms around a square with a single room on the roof for the commanding officer. Close to this gate is one of those wonderful stepped wells well-known in Gujrat but which are very rare in the Southern Maratha country. It is called the Andhar Bavdi. It is three-storied with one room on each of the lower storeys and three rooms on the top. An inscription on the central arch records its erection during the reign of the same prince. One of the principal features of the Panala Fort is a little three-storeyed tower called the Nayikin's Sajja or the dancing girl's tower, which contains a wealth of delicate stucco mouldings in the interior. The Commanding Officer's palace in the Fort is used as a Guest house by the Kolhapur State and is

(Exploration.) called the Residency. It is a tower of the style of Nayikin's Sajja and was built according to an inscription on it by one Maqsud Aqa during the reign of Ibrahim Adil Shah II in 1000 A.H.—1591 A.D. One of the largest reservoirs built on the top of a hill is to be found at Panala. The dam was built in 964 A.H.—1556 A.D. by one Malik Jafar, during the reign of Ibrahim Adil Shah I. The celebrated temple of Ambâbâi in Panala is surrounded by a number of older shrines. One of these is the temple of the nine planets. The ceiling of its porch is divided into nine sunken panels each of which bears a representation of a planet. Another temple is a Digambara Jaina temple, now occupied by an image of Vishṇu as *Śeshaśâyin*. Below the dome of the Maṇḍapa is a frieze consisting of a number of nude Jaina figures each standing under an arch.

About four miles from the railway station of Landhi on the North-Western Railway and not more than fifteen miles from the city of Karachi stands a curious little monument which seems to be an unusual form of Buddhist *stūpa*. The structure is comprised of three different parts. The lowest is a stepped pyramid, consisting of nine steps; the middle section is a spheroid with a circular cross-section; while the finial, which is fitted into the topmost slab of the middle section by a mortice and tenon arrangement, is an elaborately carved block of stone. The stepped plinth is built of ashlar masonry with a rubble core. The stones of the first eight steps are dressed on the outer side, but are devoid of decoration. The sixth layer which like the eighth is octagonal in outline, shows a deeply carved surface decoration composed of simple geometrical patterns. The middle section, which was described above as being spheroidal in shape, consists of well-fitted slabs and has probably a hollow or rubble core. The finial has also deeply carved, geometrical designs like those with which the tombs on the Chaukhandi Hill are decorated. The structure stands on a small mound along the bank of a river, and is entirely above ground. No inscription is found on it.

Southern Circle. Mr. Longhurst reports that he was unable in the year under review to undertake any excavation, for lack of time. But the second part of his Provincial Report for 1917-18 contains a long and valuable account of the remarkable temple complex at Srisailam, in the inaccessible forests of the Nallamalai Hills in the north-east portion of the Nandikotkur taluk of the Kurnool District. Mr. Longhurst notes that of the total distance of 25 miles between Nagaluti and Srisailam, at least eight miles of the way is either paved with huge stone slabs, or else provided with flights of steps up and down the steep hill sides, a truly remarkable feature, eloquent of the importance attaching to this monument in by-gone centuries. The history and origin of this temple, which is dedicated to Siva in the form of Mallikarjuna, are both more obscure than we should like. The lithic records preserved at the site do not, Mr. Longhurst tells us, (quoting Mr. Krishna Shastri), carry us farther back than the 14th century A.D., as the oldest of the epigraphs refer to the Kakatiya king Prataparudradeva, who was ruling the Telugu country at that time. "The stone steps leading down to the river" (here called the Patalaganga) "were constructed by the famous Reddi king Vema Reddi, in the beginning of the 14th century, and repaired by a Kadamba Princess named Vitthalamba at the end of that century. Another inscription records that Annavema Reddi, a son of Vema Reddi, built a hall or *maṇḍapa* for heroes (Vira) in the temple courtyard. It was called the *Virasiromaṇḍapa*, *i.e.*, the hall for the heads of heroes, and we are informed that in this *maṇḍapa* hosts of Konga Viras, excited by religious fervour, cut off their heads and tongues and offered them as votive offerings to the god." The Vijayanagar kings of the 15th century greatly improved the temple, and certain of their records exist. But the only actual proofs of an antiquity greater than the 14th are references in other places and in literature, which go to show that Srisailam was already known in the Gupta period at least, though it may of course be older still. The monumental remains, however, are not assignable to any much earlier period than the epigraphs. Mr. Longhurst has published a useful plan, as No. 4 of his 16 very interesting plates. The inner courtyard containing the main temple buildings is surrounded with a lofty wall, some 22 feet high, measuring about 500 feet from east to west, and 600 from north to south. "The gateways," Mr. Longhurst says, "are of the usual kind common to the Vijayanagara period, to which they no doubt belong." The Mallikarjuna Temple itself stands in the middle of the inner court, and is surrounded by a number of minor shrines. It is a small, stone-built structure, consisting of a cella about ten feet square facing the east, and enshrining a stone linga. In front of the shrine doorway, which is handsomely carved, is the *mukha maṇḍapa* or pillared hall with its three side porches, which was constructed by the Vijayanagara king Harihara II in A.D. 1404-05. It contains some handsome stone pillars, doorframes, and ornamental stone eaves, but Mr. Longhurst says that otherwise there is nothing remarkable about its architecture. One remarkable feature of it, however, is that the stepped tower over the shrine chamber, the door-frames and eaves of the pillared hall in front of it, together with the figures of bulls which decorate the roof, were originally all encased in copper gilt plates and embossed ornaments of the same material. Most of these have now disappeared, but a few specimens illustrated with Mr. Longhurst's report show what a loss this has involved. There are said to be seven specimens preserved in the Madras Museum now. Some of these, as well as certain metal images found by Mr. Longhurst still at the site, reach a high level of artistic achievement, but although these are artistically the most excellent of the art products here, they are perhaps less valuable to the antiquarian than the wonderful bas-reliefs carved upon the surface of the high enclosing wall. Mr. Longhurst publishes several of these compositions, and discusses them at length, from which it appears that a complete publication of this material would constitute a remarkably interesting contribution to the study of Hindu iconography. The occurrence here, as at Konarak, in Orissa, of what seems to be the African giraffe, is a surprising feature, repeated, so I have recently learned from the Honourable Mr. Best, in certain cave paintings in the Hoshangabad District of the Central Provinces. But whether these figures do actually represent the giraffe is a matter of some uncertainty.

Another monument discussed in Mr. Longhurst's report at some length is the famous Kapotesvara temple at Chezarla in the Guntur District, in which we have, preserved as a Hindu temple, one of the very few structural Buddhist

(Exploration.) chaityas known to exist in India. The peculiar features of the building are well shown in the illustrative plates and the plan which accompany the report in question.

Bihar and Orissa. Nalanda.

In the Eastern Circle the excavation of the famous monasteries and stupas at Nalanda, north of Rajgir in the Patna District of Bihar, was continued. At Site No. 1, the most southerly of the big monastic complexes, the clearance effected this season was more external than heretofore, part of the east side and the main south wall of the monastery being set free in part. Inside the enclosure, the northern stretch of the lowermost verandah on the east was freshly excavated, and yielded a considerable quantity of antiquities ranging from large sculptural figures to small seals; and the corner on the north-east was turned and progress made in clearing the north verandah of the monastery on this level to about its middle point. As has been recorded before, it had been found that through the ages at least four monastic quadrangles had been erected on this same site, and the verandah cleared in this and the preceding seasons was supposed to be the oldest of the series. Trial digging last winter, however, has now proved that a fifth and still older structure occurs deeper down. But no approach to this is possible as yet. Meanwhile the verandah of the lowest level reached last year continues to be the richest portion of the site in the matter of finds, and those recovered this season were not inferior in interest to those met with earlier. A surprising number of metal images, of all sizes, have come to light, (*cf.* Fig. *a* of Plate XIV), and what seem to be portions of chain armour now corroded into shapeless masses. The real nature as well as the explanation of these curious and unexpected objects remain problematic.

At site No. 3, the large stupa mound west of Site No. 1, excavation was continued on the west half of the north side, the corner was turned at the north-west, and clearance effected to practically all but the southern end of the façade on this west side. As was to have been expected, a large number of small stupas were found clustering around the main stupa, but those on the west are more plentiful than on the sides heretofore examined, and disclose at least three definite strata, with what now seems a still later level represented by a pavement laid across certain stupas in the uppermost stratum of the three. A few sculptural fragments were recovered in this general area this season, including the interesting and as yet problematic piece illustrated by Fig. *b* of Plate XIV. The large and very fine figure of Avalokitesvara shown in Fig. *c* of the same Plate was found near the surface north of the main stupa. The seated Buddha with inscribed halo shown in Fig. *d* was found the year before. A visit paid to Nalanda by Sir John Marshall in January 1918 led to his giving a special grant-in-aid from Imperial funds amounting to Rs. 2,000, and this money was applied principally to opening new soil. To this end a single trench, illustrated by Figs. *a* and *b* of Plate XV, was led from the central point of the most southerly stupa (Site III) due north to the central point of the high mound on the extreme north, thus crossing all the big mounds which constitute the line of stupas on the west of the ancient area. This new trench laid bare sections of each of the stupas crossed,

a. NALANDA: BRONZE STATUETTE OF BUDDHA (No. 417 FROM SITE I).

b. NALANDA: STATUETTE No. 61 FROM SITE III.

c. NALANDA. AVALOKITESVARA (No. 83 FROM SITE III).

d. NALANDA: SEATED BUDDHA (No. 54 FROM SITE III).

a. NALANDA: LONG TRENCH LOOKING S FROM MOUND B.

b. NALANDA: LONG TRENCH LOOKING N FROM MOUND B.

Photo-engraved & printed at the offices of the Survey of India, Calcutta, [illegible]

Fig. 1.

Fig. 2.

Fig. 3.

Fig. 4.

PATALIPUTRA EXCAVATIONS: TERRACOTTA FIGURINES FROM BULANDI BAGH.

and disclosed the fact that the northernmost is faced with somewhat elaborate brick ornament, differing on each of its four sides. A certain number of small stupas and other foundations came to light in the body of the trench also, and one of these shows seated stucco figures in niches. But the extent of this new digging, some 1,500 feet in length by 35 feet in width, prevented anything beyond surface clearance this season. It has, however, opened up in a preliminary way, a tract of great interest and no less promise, and when excavation can be resumed, it is anticipated that finds will multiply. Until the end of the war, however, no more excavation, as such, will be undertaken. The conservation of the excavated remains, which was begun in earnest this past season, will be pushed on, to ensure the safety of the structures. But only works of an urgent nature will be taken up even in this case, in conformity with the general principles laid down by Sir John Marshall for the remaining period of the war. **(Exploration.)**

Owing to the absence of the Superintendent from Patna in the summer, no further work was done in the season under review at Pataliputra, but Plate XVI illustrates some of the extraordinarily interesting terracotta figurines recovered in the Bulandi Bagh portion of Sir Ratan Tata's excavations, which have not been hitherto published. They were all found in the dark blue soil enveloping the ancient wooden rampart, and their extreme antiquity is manifest, even apart from the evidence of findspot. The delightful realism of the smiling infant's head shown in Fig. 2 is exceptional if not unique in early India. PATALIPUTRA

Mr. Taw Sein Ko informs me that "No excavation was undertaken in Burma during the year. Reports were received, however, from time to time, from District officers of archæological finds made in their districts. The most interesting among these is a bronze figure representing the goddess Tārā Dēvī (Figs. 1 and 2 of Plate XVII), which was found among the débris while digging around an old and ruined temple near Manawgōn village in the Myothit Township of the Magwe District. She is represented as seated cross-legged on a lotus throne, with her right hand in the charity *mudrā*, while her left holds by its stem the long stalk of a blue lotus (*utpala*). She wears anklets, bracelets, armlets, a necklace, earrings and a crown, and her hair is done up into a knot at the back of her head in the fashion of the South Indian coiffure. The anatomy of the figure, especially its deep navel, slender waist, and well-developed bosom, indicates its Indian origin. Judging by similar figures found in Nipal, this figure of Tārā Dēvī may be ascribed to the 9th—10th century A.D., *i.e.*, two or three centuries earlier than the terra-cotta votive tablets with which it was found. Its total height with the throne is 3 inches. In the paintings, as well as in the figures in bronze, which have hitherto been discovered in Burma, only the gods of the Mahāyāna pantheon are represented as principal figures, the most prominent being Padmapāni or the Lotus bearer, which is a non-Tantric form of Avalokitēsvara. The goddesses, where they are represented, assume only a subordinate position as consorts of the gods and in juxtaposition to the latter. In the present instance, the goddess is represented alone and as occupying an independent position, and it is, no doubt, a definite proof of the reproductive or female principle being admitted into Mahāyānism, which is utterly absent in the Southern School. **Burma.**

(Exploration.) "Pagan is not only the home of various styles of religious architecture, but is also the greatest store-house of sculptures and painting. Native chroniclers affirm that Pagan was founded in 108 A.D. on the break-up of the Empire at Prome, but researches hitherto made into its ancient history have not been able to confirm the statement with any degree of certainty. Authentic history, based on architecture, and lithic records, begins only with the 11th century A.D., *i.e.*, with the reign of Anawrata (1044-1077 A.D.). Foreign influence, chiefly South-Indian, appears to have been predominant during his reign, and the reign of Kyanzittha (1084-1112), his successor. Indian sculptors and artists appear to have been imported through Thaton and Pegu. Traces of foreign influence gradually disappeared till by the end of the 12th century A.D., art and architecture became Burmanized and indigenous. This period synchronizes with the establishment of Muhammadan power in India and with the cessation of the overflow of cultural influences from that centre to Burma. As an illustration of this fact, I have selected photographs of three stone sculptures found at Pagan, each one of which represents the period to which it belongs (Plate XVII, Figures 3-5).

"Figure 3 is a stone tablet, measuring about 3 feet in height, found among the ruins of a temple at Wetkyi-in which is situated mid-way between Pagan and Nyaung-u. It represents the Buddha in the *dharmachakra mudrā* seated cross-legged on a lotus throne. It is an image of the Sage in alto-relievo recalling the sculptures of later mediæval Gupta art. Its sharp and almost Caucasian features—oval face, broad and high forehead, aquiline nose, small determined mouth, pointed up-turned chin, broad and protruding chest, big and well developed arms, and slender waist—are decidedly Indian, and its close-fitting drapery is strongly reminiscent of the Gupta or Northern Indian style, which was much influenced by the Greek School of Art in Gandhāra. An attempt was made to repeat these features on the next figure (figure 4), which is found in the Ananda Pagoda, but a glance will show that it is not very successful. The expression has lost its pleasing vivacity and has become conventional; the face has become round and the pointed up-turned chin, which denotes a spirit of enquiry, is absent; the chest is still protruding and the upper and lower limbs are still abnormally developed, but the legs from the knees downwards are very slender and weak; and the anatomy is less perfect. The figure in the Ananda Pagoda is decidedly based on South Indian or Dravidian models, in contra-distinction to the North-Indian or Gupta models. The transition from an Indian to a Mongolian type becomes more pronounced in figure 5. Instead of a figure with sharp fine features, we see one with a short thick-set body and heavy expression. The tradition in Burmese iconography that the facial type and anatomy of a Buddha figure resemble those of that particular generation and particular community which set it up, finds a fitting example in the above images. Figure 3 was set up about 1057 A.D., *i.e.*, before the conquest of Thaton by Anawrata, which heralded Dravidian influences into Pagan, and figures 4 and 5 in 1090 and 1196 A.D. respectively. Figure 4 forms one of a series of sculptures in the Ananda Pagoda,[1] which is certainly a fabric constructed

[1] *Vide* Plates XXXI—XXXVII of the Archæological Survey of India Annual Report, 1913-14, Part II.

TĀRĀ DEVĪ.

FIG. 1. FRONT VIEW. FIG. 2. BACK VIEW.

FIG. 3. BUDDHA FOUND IN A RUINED TEMPLE AT WETKYI-IN, PAGAN.

FIG. 4. BUDDHA IN THE ANANDA PAGODA, PAGAN

FIG. 5. BUDDHA IN THE DAMAYAZIKA PAGODA, PAGAN.

Photo-engraved & printed at the Offices of the Survey of India, Calcutta, [illegible]

by Dravidian architects and sculptors, and figure 5 is found in the Damayazika pagoda which was built by King Narapatisithu in 1196 A.D." (Exploration.)

H. E. H. the Nizam's dominions.

Mr. Yazdani, Superintendent of Archæology in His Exalted Highness the Nizam's Dominions, reports that during his tour in the Adilabad District, in January 1918, he discovered two *vihara* caves at Mahur, on which he subsequently published a short note in the Journal of the Hyderabad Archæological Society. Mr. Yazdani says :—" The front of the main cave has fallen down, but its interior is intact, and consists of a double hall (77′ 6″×47′) and a sanctuary (19′×18′ 6″) surrounded with a *pradakshina*. The lintel of the shrine door is adorned with Brahmanical images and pediments of the Dravidian order; and two gigantic sculptures of Dvarapalas, cut with considerable grace and beauty, stand at either side of the door. It is difficult to fix with any certainty the age of the cave, but from its general style, it appears to have been excavated about the same time as the later Brahmanical caves at Ellora, that is to say, between the 7th and the 9th centuries of the Christian era. The other cave is unfinished, but its plan is worked out in the rock. The cave when finished would have comprised an outer hall with a row of pillars in the front and small rooms at the eastern and western ends and an inner hall divided into two aisles and flanked with small rooms on the eastern and western sides. The shrine with the *pradakshina* would have been at the southern end of the inner hall."

Museums.

Sir John Marshall's report on the working of the Archæological Section of the Indian Museum will be found in Appendix E of this report. The cataloguing of the Archæological specimens in the Bijapur Museum has been completed. At the Lucknow Museum the work of labelling in the Epigraphical Section and Brahmanical Gallery was finished, and the antiquities discovered at Sankisa last year were arranged in cases in the Saheth-Maheth room, which is shortly to be opened to the public. The services of the Archæological Chemist were lent to the Lahore Museum for two months in order that he might clean and preserve a number of antiquities. Both the Muttra and Peshawar Museums are feeling the need of expansion. At the former the Honorary Curator complains that many of the antiquities are deteriorating for want of sufficient accommodation and at the latter many specimens have to be stored in boxes. It is to be hoped that the matter of enlarging these two museums may be taken up as soon as possible after the war.

Fresh acquisitions.

New acquisitions to the Archæological Section of the Indian Museum will be found in Appendix E. The Mathura Museum heads the list with the largest list of fresh acquisitions, *viz.*, 196. Most of the specimens came from three excavations at Girdharpur Tila, Gayatri Tila and Bajna. 41 specimens were added to the Lucknow Museum, 70 to the Lahore, (of which 40 are on loan) and 39 to the Delhi Museum. The Madras Museum received 9 new acquisitions, the Peshawar Museum 2, Ajmer Museum 14, Bijapur Museum 46, Quetta 3 and Gwalior 12. Four sets of copperplate inscriptions recording grants are among the acquisitions made by the Madras Museum. Some Rs. 2,500 was expended on the purchase of antiquities, for the Delhi Museum, among the most important of the acquisitions being a manuscript copy of the Shah Nama in two volumes; three *farmans* of Aurengzeb, one each of Shahjahan, Muhammad Shah and Dara Shikoh,

(Exploration.) and two Ghori plates. The acquisitions of most interest in the Lahore Museum are an illustrated Persian Manuscript of the five works of the Poet Nizami written in the latter part of the 15th century and 24 paintings on paper or cloth illustrating passages from the Markandeya and Chandi. The most important of the new acquisitions in the Lucknow Museum are five very well preserved Buddhist sculptures from Mahoba in the Hamirpur District.

Archæological Chemist.

The Archæological Chemist was called to Taxila to examine and take in hand the preservation of the various objects excavated there. The stuccoes, on chemical examination, were found to contain only a negligible quantity of injurious salts; therefore it is hoped that they will remain unaltered under ordinary atmospheric conditions. They retain a good hard surface but the damaged parts have revealed a softer skeleton which will be hardened by means of "Fluates," Hydrofluosilicic acid, Colloidal silica, or the Baryta treatment, as soon as these materials can be procured from England. The terracottas and pottery also are free from injurious salts, with the exception of those from Sirkap and the Bir Mound which contained these in a small quantity. They are being eliminated by steeping in plain water. Stone and terracottas covered with hard calcareous incrustations are being cleaned with a very weak Hydrochloric Acid solution followed by thorough washing in plain water. Incrustations from partly baked clay seals were freed by careful burning in a muffle furnace. The necessary hardening of semi-baked clay seals and other similar soft material was obtained by impregnation with a thin bleached-shellac solution in alcohol. Decayed bone and ivory have been strengthened by impregnation with thin hot gelatin followed by formaline. The glass only required washing with plain water. The repair of stone is being done by means of Meyer's Cement while that of terracottas and glass with shellac varnish. The iron objects are being preserved by the Blell and Krefting methods, while bronzes having a sound metallic core are freed from incrustations by reduction with zinc and caustic soda solution; they are thoroughly washed first in ordinary and then with distilled water, and finally coated with hard paraffin-wax.

The Archæological Chemist stayed at Taxila for about seven weeks finishing the treatment of 520 objects. Others requiring more elaborate treatment were taken to his laboratory at Calcutta.

Treasure Trove.

51 Treasure Trove finds of coins were reported during the year under review and comprised about 9160 specimens. 3976 coins came from the United Provinces, 3466 from Bihar and Orissa, 602 from Bombay, 463 from the North West Frontier Province, 193 from the Central Provinces, 163 from Rajputana, 98 each from Assam and Gwalior and 86 from Bengal. There were no coins of any extraordinary interest though a few rare specimens have been reported. A find of silver punch marked coins was recovered in Palampur, but a detailed report on them has not been received.

Epigraphy.

Of the finds other than coins little of interest has been brought to notice.

Rao Sahib H. Krishna Sastri, Officer in charge of the current duties of the Government Epigraphist for India, writes as follows:—

"Two parts of the *Epigraphia Indica*, viz., Part VIII of Volume XII and

Part IV of Volume XIII, were issued under the editorship of Dr. Sten Konow who after this, passed on his charge to Dr. Thomas of the India Office, London. Under the latter's editorship Parts V and VI of Volume XIII were issued in July 1917 but on account of the delay in the receipt of facsimile plates from Messrs. W. Griggs and Sons, London, these were sent out by the Press only in June 1918. The one general impression which the reader is likely to form in running his eye through the pages of these parts, is the unusually large number of printer's mistakes which they contain. Apparently these are due to various causes, the irregular postal service and delay caused by the war, being the most prominent. **(Epigraphy)**

"The Epigraphical work done during the year in the different Archæological Circles and in the Museums of Calcutta, Lucknow and Ajmer, may next be briefly examined. A note on the Hathigumpha inscription of Kharavela has been published by Mr. R. D. Banerji in the Journal of the Bihar and Orissa Research Society Vol. III, Part IV. Mr. Prayag Dayal, Officiating Curator of the Lucknow Museum, has contributed a paper to the *Epigraphia Indica*—not yet published—on the interesting Poona copper-plates of the Vakataka queen Prabhavati-gupta, recently brought to light by Professor K. B. Pathak. It is made out to be the earliest copper-plate grant of the Gupta Period, and proving the close connection of the Vakatakas of Berar with the imperial Guptas, the age of the former dynasty is fixed once for all. Two copper-plates found at Garra, in Chhatarpur State, are also taken up for examination by Mr. Prayag Dayal and a paper on them is under preparation. The Ajmer Museum has copied 12 inscriptions of which a brief abstract is given on page 2 of the Annual Report on the working of that institution for the year ending 31st March 1918. All are found on the pedestals of images both Hindu and Jaina, and give the dates when these images were installed or when the temple containing them was built. A really interesting discovery is the *Mahakavya Rajaprasasti* of 24 cantos found inscribed on 25 slabs on the dam of the Rajasamudra lake in Mewar. We know of other poetical works also inscribed on stones. The *Harakeli-Nataka*, for instance, by Vigraharajadeva of Sakambhari was one of this kind (*Ind. Ant.*, Vol. XIX, p. 210*f*). So also was *Lalita-Vigraharajanataka* (*ibid* pp. 205*ff*.). The *Parijatamanjari-Natika* of Madana and the two Prakrit poems at Dhar ascribed to king Bhoja, also inscribed on stone, are published in Volume VIII of the *Epigraphia Indica*. But this *Rajaprasasti* is a unique record, the only one so far discovered in India where such a large work of no less than 24 cantos is inscribed on stone. The contents of these cantos are briefly noted by Mr. Gaurishankar H. Ojha and are of great interest and value for the history of the times. The enormous lake of Rajasamudra built by king Rajasimha appears to have been the central theme of the poem. Around this were spun numerous other incidents, the genealogies of kings, their battles, peace negotiations, royal amenities, ceremonies, pilgrimages, charities and gifts. Such a poem cannot but be without its peculiar interest to students of history and Mr. Ojha must be congratulated on the discovery of such a fine record.

"The only Epigraphical discovery made in the Frontier Circle was an inscribed copper relic casket, the property of one of the sons of the Nawab of Landi.

(Epigraphy.) It is stated to have come from the Kurram valley and is shaped like a miniature *stupa* with *harmika* and umbrellas, all complete. The inscription consists of four lines in the Kharoshthi script of the 2nd century A.D. punctured on the four sides of the base of the casket and is dated on the 20th day of the month of Asvina, the year being doubtful. In the opinion of Mr. V. Natesa Aiyar, Archæological Superintendent, Frontier Circle, the record refers to the enshrinement of relics of the Buddha Sakyamuni in a monument belonging to the Sarvastivadins. Pandit Daya Ram Sahni reports from the Northern Circle that during the year under review were copied and deciphered about 200 inscriptions of which 154 come from Deogarh in the Jhansi district. Three of the inscriptions are in the Brahmi characters of the Gupta period. The largest and most interesting of these latter is a seven-line inscription at Deogarh which is attached to a relief exhibiting the eight divine mothers. The rest are in Sanskrit or Hindi and are written in Nagari characters. Their chief interest lies in the help they give in dating the sculptures and the monuments on which they are engraved and some possess special value for Jaina iconography as they supply the names of twenty out of the twenty-four *Yakshis* of the Jaina pantheon. The Eastern Circle reports that no Epigraphical work was done during the year under review. In the Western Circle two copper-plates of the Kadamba kings Ravivarman and Krishnavarman dated in the 35th and 19th years of their reign respectively, were received through the kindness of Mr. S. N. Hegde of Ajjibal, North Kanara district. Two other sets which belong to the time of the Gujarat Chalukya king Karna and are in possession of an illiterate peasant, have been photographed. A set of three copper-plates presented by the Bhavnagar Darbar to the Prince of Wales Museum, Bombay, are found on examination to contain a record of the Valabhi king Dhruvasena I, issued in the Gupta-Valabhi Era 210 (A.D. 528-29). Another Valabhi grant on a single plate of the Gupta-Valabhi year 206 (A.D. 524-25) was also examined at Baroda by Dr. Sukthankar, the Assistant Archæological Superintendent, Western Circle. A short stone inscription at Sanchi examined by the Superintendent himself has proved to be a very interesting one inasmuch as it is likely to provide a date and a location for Svami Jivadaman the father of Swami Rudrasimha II the founder of the third Dynasty of satraps in Saurashtra. The inscription in the opinion of Mr. R. D. Banerji bears the date in two numerical symbols which are interpreted as 200 and 1, mentions a Saka (Scythian) general or judge named Sridharavarman and opens with a eulogy of Skanda the commander of the celestial army.

"In the Southern Circle were copied and examined the largest number of inscriptions on record which throw a flood of light on the political, economic, social and religious history of Southern India. In all 876 new stone inscriptions, each in size ten times as big as an average North Indian inscription, have been deciphered, and 22 copper-plate inscriptions examined. The Brahmi inscriptions in the Caves of Southern India have long failed to attract the attention they deserve from scholars of Archæology and Epigraphy. These were tackled once again, and Mr. Ramaprasad Chanda of the Varendra Research Society, who had been deputed by the Director General to study South-Indian Epigraphy, was given an opportunity to look into these curious records which still continue to puzzle the antiquarian. It is hoped that the results of Mr. Chanda's preliminary study will soon appear in the pages of the *Epigraphia Indica* and open the way, however slightly it may be, for their proper interpretation and enquiry. With this object in view the South-Indian Epigraphist visited the Caves of Madura and Tinnevelly with Mr. Chanda and prepared careful readings directly from the stone and took fresh estampages discovering also on this same tour some more inscriptions of a similar type in the Siddharmalai cavern at Mettuppatti. (Epigraphy.)

"The copper-plates examined during the year supply much interesting information about the Early Eastern Chalukyan kings, the Bhanjas of Khinjali and the Eastern Gangas. One of the sets belongs to the time of Sarvasiddhi Jayasimha I whose records are very rare. Another supplies the date Saka 814 (A.D. 892) for the coronation of Chalukya-Bhima I, which is 4 years in advance of that arrived at by Dr. Fleet in his Eastern Chalukya Chronology. A stone record of his 17th year which has been copied at Bezwada mentions the foundation of the Parthisvara temple on the Indrakila Hill, by a certain Chattapa. A copper-plate of the time of Saktivarman supplies some historical facts hitherto unknown. It mentions among the enemies of Vijayaditya III not only Mangi and Sankila but also a certain Baddega who is identified with the Western Chalukya prince Baddiga. A son of Chalukya-Bhima I is stated to have planted a pillar of victory at Viraja which is evidently identical with Virajapuri mentioned in connection with Kollabhiganda-Vijayaditya IV at p. 118 of the Annual Report on Epigraphy for 1917. Danarnava held the title Raja-Narayana and his son Saktivarman became famous even in his youth by a victory over the Cholas and by putting to flight a certain Badyema-Maharaja. A Chola-Bhima met with his death like Ravana at the hands of this Chalukya-Narayana. Chalukya-Narayana like Chalukya-Chandra must have been a title of Saktivarman. A stone inscription of Vimaladitya found in a cavern at Ramatirtham gives him the titles Rajamartanda and Mummadi-Bhima the latter of which was already known from his Ranastipundi plates (*Ep. Ind.* Vol. VI, p. 350), and further suggests that Vimaladitya as an emperor must have also patronised Jainism and adopted as his *guru* the Jaina teacher Trailokyayogi-Siddhantadeva of the Desi-Gana.

"One of the Eastern Ganga copper-plates examined, purports to have been issued in the 342nd year of the Ganga Era by Rajendravarman son of Anantavarman; the Alamanda plates which are dated in G.E. 304 belong to the time of Anantavarman son of Rajendravarman; and thus the two records together supply three generations of kings in successive order. Another set of copper-plates from Mandasa which are dated in Saka 976, belong to the time of Anantavarman-Vajrahasta VI and mention Ranaka Sri-Dharmakhedi of the Kadamba family. Three Bhanja kings—Netribhanjadeva *alias* Kalyanakalasa, Vidyadharabhanjadeva *alias* Avaryakalasa and Yasabhanjadeva son of Rayabhanja, are represented in the collection of copper-plates.

"The Chola and Pandya records, as should be expected, preponderate in the Epigraphical collection of the Southern Circle. Several inscriptions of the Early Chola king Parantaka I (A.D. 907) are found at Kuttalam in the extreme

(Epigraphy.) south-west of the Pandya country and establish beyond doubt the conquest of the whole of the Pandya dominion claimed for him in the Udayendiram grant. Rajendra-Chola I, another famous Chola emperor, actually constructed a huge palace at Madura and there stationed his son Chola-Pandya as the Viceroy of the Pandyan kingdom. South-Indian temples as centres of educational institutions have been often referred to in inscriptions. In the current year has been copied at Ennayiram in the South Arcot district a record of extraordinary interest which gives full details about the establishment of a college and hostel where about 350 students were taught the Veda, Vedanta, Vyakarana, Prabhakara, Mimamsa and the Rupavatara. The discovery of another valuable epigraph supplies a hitherto missing chapter of the Tamil sacred hymns called *Devaram* which in the 12th century A.D. was collected by the hagiologist Sekkilar with the apology that he was not able to collect the whole of the writings of the saints but only a portion thereof. As many as 190 inscriptions belong to the later Pandya kings of Tinnevelly. After four successive generations from Arikesari Parakrama to Parakrama-Kulasekhara, *i.e.*, after 1503 A.D. the Southern Pandya country seems to have been overrun by the Travancore chiefs Udayamartandavarman and Ramavarman and to have remained in their possession for about 30 years when again it was recovered by Srivallabha Kulasekhara, hence styled 'the reviver of the old time.'

"Coming to the Vijayanagara dynasties, we find two inscriptions of the time of Devaraya II which are of much interest for the economic history of the country. The two main divisions of the cultivating classes, *viz.*, the *Valangai* and the *Idangai* being tired of the oppressive measures of taxation adopted by the officials, formed themselves into a constitutional assembly to resist the exactions and resolved not to pay more than what was reasonable. One of these supplies the actual rates of taxes settled by the assembly of the people and the several classes of professions. During the reign of the Saluvas who stepped in at the close of the first Vijayanagara dynasty, there were similar troubles in the matter of taxation and people resolved to leave the country in a body. The disabilities were at once removed and the ancient rights restored. The standard measuring rod was also then changed from 18 to 20 feet, thereby reducing in effect the taxes on lands, checking theft and ruin and raising the people to a flourishing condition.

"Among the miscellaneous inscriptions secured by the Southern Circle may be noted two of Chola-Maharaja and Mangi-Chola in archaic characters of about the 9th century A.D. These kings must have belonged to a branch of the Early Cholas whose inscriptions have been found in the Cuddapah district and to whose country the Chinese traveller Hiuen Tsiang gave the name Chuliye. A copper-plate grant of the 12th century A.D. belongs to Sambhu-Chola, a Chola chief of the Telugu country, who claims to have ruled over the whole country between Nellur and Kalingaka. In the 50th year of his reign he is said to have defeated the king of Kalinga at Pithapuri and to have installed his two sons as *Yuvarajas*. Two of his provincial officers were Periya-Samburaya and Chiriya-Samburaya. Two records from the Madura district supply a genealogical account of 25 generations of Chenji chiefs down to Varadappa-Nayaka (A.D. 1670-71) and state that these first migrated to Vijayanagara from Maninagapura in Aryavarta about the end of the 14th century A.D. The latest record in the Southern collection is a copper-plate grant of the 17th century A.D. of the Golconda Kutb Shahi king Abdul Hassan. It mentions his two famous Brahmana ministers Akkanna and Madanna and the former's deputy Lingoji-Pandita who was ruling the Penugonda province. The inscription is highly interesting on account of the details which it supplies about a huge representative assembly in which were merchants, heads of religious institutions, village headmen, accountants, cultivators, Brahmanas, smiths, potters, weavers, tailors, washermen, hunters, barbers and shoemakers. (Epigraphy.)

"The Epigraphical work done in Burma mainly coincided with that of the new Journal *Epigraphia Burmanica*, the first number of which containing the Pali, Pyu, Talaing and Burmese versions of the Myazedi inscriptions of 1112 A.D. is expected to be published before the expiry of the current official year.[1] A re-examination of the earliest Pali records of Burma so far discovered, *viz.*, the Maunggun gold plates (*Ep. Ind.* Vol. V, p. 101*f*) and the Bawbawgyi Pagoda inscription together with the Urn inscriptions published by Mr. C. O. Blagden (*Ibid.* Vol. XII, p. 127*ff*) has enabled Mr. Taw Sein Ko to state that long before the Burmese character was in vogue there was in Burma a character closely resembling the Kadamba script of South India which is probably the progenitor of the Burmese alphabet. This is not unlikely but the latest researches in this direction tend to show that the Pallavas must have carried their script and civilization over the sea to the further east.

"The forthcoming first part of the *Epigraphia Burmanica* promises to be a very interesting one and will consist of several inscriptions of the time of the king Kyanzittha who was in friendly intercourse with a certain Choli or Chola prince, who had established himself at Kadaram or Pegu. Kyanzittha of Pagan was the third king in succession after Anawrata and ruled from 1084 to 1112 A.D. His lineage has been one of the vexed questions in Burmese history. While some believe his mother to have been an Indian princess of Vesali-Basarh in India, Mr. Taw Sein Ko holds strongly the view that this Vesali mentioned in Burmese history in connection with Anawrata is not the Vesali of India but that of Arakan as now clearly established by some Arakanese manuscripts brought to light by Maung San Shwe Bu. Kyanzittha's statue in the Ananda temple shows an Indian cast of features and there has been always a strong strain of Indian blood in the Arakanese. Kyanzittha's description in one of the Myazedi inscriptions as *Udiccadittavamsajo* (the offspring of the Northern solar family) fits in appropriately with Phayre's account of the Chandra kings of Vesali in Arakan who held Brahmanical doctrines and claimed to be of high caste. Mr. Taw Sein Ko identifies the Chola friend of Kyanzittha with Kulottunga Rajendra-Chola II who ruled from 1070 to 1118 A.D. Further investigation will have yet to prove if this Rajendra-Chola resided at Pegu or Kadaram, visited Pagan with tributes to Kyanzittha, presented his daughter and was himself converted to Buddhism by his friend the Buddhist king. Among other

[1] Volume I, Part I appeared in December 1919. The second part and the next two volumes are in the Press.

(Epigraphy.) interesting points in the Burma Report which deserve to be noted may be mentioned the reference to Vidyanagar or Vijayanagar in the Talaing poem called *Lik Smin Asah* and the classification of the various types of architecture prevailing in Pagan one of which is based on South-Indian models."

Muslim Epigraphy. The Government Epigraphist for Moslem Inscriptions, Mr. Ghulam Yazdani reports that during the year, with the co-operation of the Archæological Superintendents of the various circles, a large number of early Muslim records were copied, the majority of which are to be included in the ensuing number of the *Epigraphia Indo-Moslemica*, which is now in the press and will be published shortly. The first article in this number is by Mr. H. Beveridge, I.C.S. (Retd.), in which he has discussed the authenticity of the story about a plot to place one Mahdī Khwāja on the throne. at Babur's death, in supersession of the claims of the lawful heir, Humāyūn. The story is accepted by Abul Faẓl and other writers, and Mr. Beveridge finds no reason to discredit it and supports the view adumbrated by Mrs. Beveridge that Muḥammad Zaman (son-in-law of Babur) and not Mahdī Khwāja was the person in favour of whom the plot was planned. The most interesting part of the paper is the inscriptions, the interpretations of some of which have been full of difficulties owing to their enigmatical arrangement.

The Government Epigraphist himself has contributed four articles to this number. The first of these is a short paper on two inscriptions in Ẓafar Khān's mosque at Tribeni, which were assigned by Blochmann to the beginning of the eighth century of the Hijra. Mr. Yazdani has deciphered the date of the inscriptions (913 A.H.) and has critically studied their phraseology, script and contents. In another essay he has dealt with two records from Petlad, a taluqa in the Baroda district of His Highness the Gaekwad's territory. One of them is dated 633 A. H.: it is the earliest Muslim record in the Bombay Presidency. Petlad (the original name of which was Petilāpādra) was an important *parganah* of the old Gujarat Kingdom and yielded a revenue of Rs. 20,00,000. The inscription is in Arabic and is important from both literary and epigraphical points of view. The second record from Petlad is a bilingual inscription in Persian and Sanskrit of the reign of Ghiyāthu-d-dīn Tughlaq.

The other two articles by the Government Epigraphist are of importance for the study of Muslim chronology in India. One of them deals with the epitaphs of the Quṭb Shahī Kings, the dates of whose births, deaths and accession to the throne are not uniformly given in contemporary and later writings. Mr. Yazdani has discussed the subject and has affixed to his paper a chronological table of this dynasty based on mural records and contemporary writings, published and unpublished. The other essay is a comprehensive survey of all the inscriptions of the Khalji Sulṭāns of Delhi from epigraphical, artistic, literary and historical points of view. This article is a continuation of the Government Epigraphist's previous article on the inscriptions of the early Sulṭāns of Delhi and is written on the same lines.

During the year under review the same officer in his capacity as Nazim of the Archæological Department, His Exalted Highness the Nizam's Dominions, obtained facsimiles of several Bahmanī and Quṭb Shahī inscriptions in the Medak Fort. An inscription was copied at Narsāpūr which gives the name of one Khafī Khān as the builder of a well, probably identical with the great historian of this name, who was appointed Diwān by Nizamu-l-Mulk in the reign of Farrukh Siyar. This is dated 1140 A.H. (1727 A.D.) and the historian Khafī Khān died in 1144 A.H. (Epigraphy.)

In Rajputana, Dr. Tessitori has copied about 250 inscriptions, all from places in the Bikaner State, but, with a very few exceptions, these are all *sati*-tablet inscriptions, and though they may often have a considerable value in connection with the local history, they are not very important epigraphically. The only inscriptions of some size and importance which Dr. Tessitori has so far discovered in the Bikaner State, are :—(*a*) a *Kirtistambha* inscription recording the digging of a tank at Vāsī (about 15 miles S.-W. of Bikaner) by rāṇī Dūlahadevī, a daughter of rāṇā Ksema Simha (Khimv Sī) of Jāngalakūpa (Jāmg'ū) and wife of rāvala Karna Deva of Jesalmer, in Samvat 1381; (*b*) an inscription recording the repairing of the Susānī temple of Morkhānā by Surāṇā Hema Rāja in Saṁvat 1573; (*c*) a long *prasasti*-inscription caused to be engraved by rāja Rāya Simha on the jamb of the Sūraj Pol gate in the Bikaner Fort, to commemorate the founding of the said Fort in Saṁvat 1645 and the completion of the said gate in Samvat 1650; and lastly (*d*) an inscription set up by Manohara Rāya over one of the gates of the fort of Bhatner (Hanumāngadh) to commemorate the capture of the same fort by him in the Hijira year 1017. The first three inscriptions are in Sanskrit, and the last mentioned one is in Persian. Bikaner.

The tours of the Archæological Superintendents are chronicled in their respective annual reports, and need not be mentioned here. Sir John Marshall's movements embraced visits to Manshera, Kashmir, Taxila, Agra, Sanchi, Delhi, Benares, Sarnath, Calcutta, Burma, Nalanda, Patna and Khajaraha (Bundelkhand). He was encamped at Taxila for nearly two months and about a month at Sanchi in order to supervise conservation works, which were in progress at those places. Tour.

The following publications were issued during the year :— Publications.

1. Annual Report of the Director General of Archæology in India, Part I for the year 1915-16.
2. Annual Reports of the Southern, Western, Eastern, Northern, Frontier. and Burma Circles as well as the Epigraphical Report of the Assistant Archæological Superintendent for Epigraphy, Southern Circle, for the year 1916-17.
3. Report of the Archæological Section of the Indian Museum for the year 1916-17.
4. Guide to the Buddhist Ruins of Sarnath—2nd Edition.
5. Epigraphia Indica, Part 8, Vol. XII.
6. Epigraphia Indica, Parts 4 to 7, Vol. XIII and Part 1, Vol. XIV.
7. Revised List of Ancient Monuments in the Madras Presidency.
8. Catalogue of Prehistoric Antiquities in the Indian Museum.
9. Bijapur and its Architectural Remains.

In addition to the above, South Indian Inscriptions Vol. III, Part 3 was passed on to Press and Pt. 4 and a general index and introduction to Vol. III are well in hand. Vol. IV has also made good progress.

Library. 304 new volumes including periodicals were added to the Central Library, Simla, of which 126 were obtained in exchange for our own publications, 27 were received as presents and 151 were purchased.

Photographs. A list of photographic negatives prepared during the year is published in Appendix D to this Report.

Personnel. In the Southern Circle Mr. A. H. Longhurst took a month's privilege leave during which M. Ry. Rao Sahib H. Krishna Sastri Avergal, Assistant Superintendent for Epigraphy, held charge of the current duties of his office. The services of Prof. D. R. Bhandarkar having been temporarily lent to the Calcutta University, arrangements were made to fill up the post of Superintendent, Western Circle, by the appointment of Mr. R. D. Banerji, Assistant Superintendent, Indian Museum, Calcutta, Professor Bhandarkar holding charge of the Archæological Section, Indian Museum, in addition to his University duties. Mr. V. Natesa Aiyar, Superintendent, Frontier Circle, was on privilege leave from 25th April to 22nd July 1917 when his Assistant, Khan Sahib Mian Wasiuddin, held charge of the current duties of his office. Sir John Marshall was on special duty from the middle of June 1917 for a period of 4 months for the purpose of editing several archæological publications when Dr. D. B. Spooner, Superintendent in the Eastern Circle, officiated for him. Mons. Chas. Duroiselle, Assistant Archæological Superintendent for Epigraphy, Burma Circle, held charge of the Eastern Circle during Dr. Spooner's absence. Mr. G. K. Nariman, Personal Assistant to the Director General of Archæology in India, reverted to his substantive appointment on 1st April 1917, and no successor was appointed in his place. The post of Government Epigraphist for India remained vacant and Rao Sahib H. Krishna Shastri held charge of the current duties of the office. The editorship of the Epigraphia Indica was transferred from Professor Konow to Dr. F. W. Thomas, C.I.E., Librarian, India Office. The headquarters of the Eastern Circle were transferred from Calcutta to Bankipore in July 1917.

Two new additions were made to the staff of this Department during the year, *viz.*, Dr. L. P. Tessitori and Mr. Mohammad Sana Ullah. Dr. L. P. Tessitori, who has been employed for some time on a Summary Survey of the Bardic Chronicles of Rajputana, was charged in addition to his duties to compile lists of Monuments, etc., and to search for Sanskrit and other manuscripts and to purchase, if possible, such Rajput paintings as may be useful to this Department. In 1913 the Government of India decided to create an appointment of an Archæological Chemist on a pay of Rs. 300—25—500 a month for the cleaning and preservation of antiquities, and desired to appoint an Indian to the post. But, as no candidate with the necessary qualifications was available in India, they selected Mr. Sana Ullah, who had previously worked as Assistant Chemist to the Chemical Examiner, Indian Ordnance Department, at Naini Tal, and sent him to England in 1915, as a State Scholar to learn his work in the British Museum. Mr. Sana Ullah returned from England in June 1917 and was appointed Archæological

Chemist to the Government of India and temporarily located at the Indian Museum, Calcutta.

The Archæological Scholarship for Sanskrit was held by Mr. M. Ghosh, M.A. That for Persian and Arabic was offered to a Sanskrit student in view of the fact that there was little likelihood of fresh openings occurring for a Moslem Archæologist in the near future, and Professor Ramā Prasād Chanda, Assistant Master, Rajshahi Collegiate School, was selected to hold it, and joined the Department in July 1917. The Architectural Scholarships held by Messrs. G. C. Chandra and B. L. Dhama were extended for a further period of one year and the scholars were attached to the office of the Superintendent, Muhammadan and British Monuments, Northern Circle, Agra, for training. Maung Hla, B.A., continued to hold the scholarship in Burma. Scholarships.

D. B. SPOONER,
Offg. Director General of Archæology.

APPENDIX A.

Special grants-in-aid.—The following allotments were made out of the special grant of one lakh provided by the Government of India :—

	Rs.
Bombay	5,000
Punjab	5,000
United Provinces	5,000
North-West Frontier Province	7,000
Delhi	10,000
Conservation at Sanchi	13,500
Conservation (including provision of accommodation for antiquities) at Taxila	15,000
Exploration at Taxila	9,000
Purchase of antiquities	500
Library	2,000
Honorarium to Mr. F. H. Andrews for work connected with Stein collection of antiquities including establishment and contingencies	3,270
Report on Indian Observatories	3,500
Archæological Chemist's pay	3,600
" " establishment	360
" " travelling allowance and contingencies .	1,500
Special apparatus required for the Archæological Chemist . .	1,500
Translation of special manuscripts	600
Purchase of plants	300
Fittings for laboratory for Archæological Chemist	1,150
Excavations at Nalanda	3,000
Conservation at Jaulian and Moramoradu	4,000
Sir Aurel Stein's expenditure	1,500
Furniture for the Patna Museum	2,000
Conservation at Sarnath	1,000
Indian Museum	500
TOTAL .	99,780

APPENDIX B.

Expenditure on the Archæological Department for the year 1917-18.

		Rs.
Southern Circle	Archæology	18,899
	Epigraphy	22,039
Western Circle		33,510
Eastern Circle		47,680
Northern Circle	Superintendent, Hindu and Buddhist Monuments	14,955
	Superintendent, Muhammadan and British Monuments	22,039
Frontier Circle		31,165
Burma Circle		32,823
Director General of Archæology including Government Epigraphist and Epigraphist for Moslem Inscriptions		80,047
	TOTAL .	3,03,157

APPENDIX B—*contd.*

Expenditure on conservation, etc., including grants-in-aid from Imperial Revenues.

		Rs.
Madras		22,625
Bombay		37,332
Bengal		19,320
Assam		2,023
Central Provinces		13,432
Bihar and Orissa		11,628
Punjab	Hindu and Buddhist Monuments	8,423
	Muhammadan and British Monuments	28,655
United Provinces	Hindu and Buddhist Monuments	5,488
	Muhammadan and British Monuments	38,048
North-West Frontier Province		9,100
Delhi		59,940
Burma		11,302
Conservation at Sanchi		13,500
„ Taxila		24,000
	TOTAL	3,04,816

Special Charges.

	Rs.
Antiquities	449
Library	1,834
Special Apparatus for the Archæological Chemist	1,500
Laboratory fittings for the Archæological Chemist	1,086
Indian Museum contingencies	500
Furniture for the Patna Museum	2,000
Honorarium to Mr. P. H. Andrews including office establishment and contingencies	3,270
Translation of special manuscripts	390
Director General's Annual Report	4,619
Epigraphia Indica	1,531
Epigraphia Indo-Moslemica	819
Honorarium for editing Epigraphia Indica	500
Other Archæological publications	3,921
Purchase of Plants and Seeds for historical gardens	69
TOTAL	22,498

Appendix C.

Drawings and photographs prepared by the Department.

		Drawings.	Photos.
Southern Circle	Archæology	6	137
	Epigraphy	...	68
Western Circle		8	96
Eastern Circle		2	185
Northern Circle	Superintendent, Hindu and Buddhist Monuments	19	190
	Superintendent, Muhammadan and British Monuments	80	129
Frontier Circle		30	107
Burma Circle		1	100
Director General of Archæology		12	228
	Total	158	1,240

Appendix D.

List of Negatives prepared by the Office of the Director General of Archæology in India during the year 1917-18.

No.	Place and District.	Description.	Size.
1	Sanchi, Bhopal State.	Great Stupa, North gate from North-East . . .	6½×4¾
2	„	„ „ Head of Chauri bearer from the top of North gate	„
3	„	„ „ East gate from South-East . . .	„
4	„	„ „ „ „ „ North-East . . .	„
5	„	Tope III. General view from South-West . . .	„
6	„	Temple 17 and 18 view from North-East . . .	„
7	„	Gupta buildings and pillars North-East of Tope I . .	„
8	„	Temple 45. General view from West	„
9	„	Asoka pillar with bowl at Top Fragmentary . . .	„
10	„	4 Berm rails of great stupa	8½×6½
11	„	4 other Berm rails of great stupa	„
12	„	„ „ „ „ „	„
13	„	Standing statue of Bodhisattva	„
14	„	Chauri bearer	„
15	„	Standing figure torso	„
16	„	Headless figure seated on chair	„
17	„	Mayura Vidyaraja	„
18	„	Fragmentary sculpture. Lower portion of Tara . .	„
19	„	Female deity with attendants	„
20	„	Six-armed Goddess	„
21	„	Four-armed Goddess (Tara?)	„
22	„	Inscribed Sati stone near bungalow. East face . .	6½×4¾
23	„	„ „ „ West face . .	„
24	„	„ „ „ South face . .	„
25	„	2nd Sati stone near bungalow sculptured. North face .	„

APPENDIX D—*contd.*

No.	Place and District.	Description.	Size.
26	Sanchi, Bhopal State.	2nd Sati stone near bungalow sculptured. South face .	6½ × 4¾
27	"	" " " " " " West face .	"
28	"	3rd " " " " " South face .	"
29	"	4th " " " " " East face .	"
30	"	An inscribed Sati stone in the Sanchi village . . .	6½ × 8½
31	"	2nd " " " " " "	"
32	"	3rd " " " " " "	"
33	"	Survey plan of Sanchi and Nagori hills	"
34	Katasri or (Ujarkhera) Bhopal State.	An inscribed Ṣati stone East side	"
35	"	2nd " " " " "	"
36	"	3rd Sati stone sculptured	"
37-42	Gulmarg (Kashmir).	Gulmarg views	"
		RAJPUTANA.	
43	Rasisara (Bikaner State).	Sakhata devalis (Samvat 1382 and 1386)	"
44	"	" devali (Samvat 1382)	"
45	Morakhano .	Temple of Susani South-East	"
46	"	" " "	"
47	" .	" " South-West	"
8	" .	" " Two pillars in front of the cella .	"
49	" .	" " Doorway and cella with the images of Goddess	"
50	" .	Temple of Susani. Particulars of the Mandivara . .	"
51	" .	Devalis and Govardhana by the side of the temple . .	6½ × 4¾
52	" .	Three devalis and a loose sculpture near the temple of Susani	"
53	" .	The Govardhana near the temple of Susani	"
54	Kodamadesara	Kirtistambha of Kodama De (Samvat 1516) . . .	"
55	"	" " " " . . .	"

APPENDIX D—*contd.*

No.	Place and District.	Description.	Size.
56	Madeto . .	Devali, S. 12	$6\frac{1}{2}\times4\frac{3}{4}$
57	„ . .	Mahata devalis (S. 1315, 1321)	$8\frac{1}{2}\times6\frac{1}{2}$
58	Caravasa .	The Fort	„
59	Chapara . .	Mohila devalis (Samvat century 1300)	„
60	Pallu . .	Tirthakara images in the cella of the temple of Brahmni .	$6\frac{1}{2}\times4\frac{3}{4}$
61	„ . .	Loose sculptures built in the facade of the temple of Brahmni (Siva and Parvati) . .	„
62	„ . .	„ „ „ „ enclosure walls of the temple of Brahmni	$8\frac{1}{2}\times6\frac{1}{2}$
63	„ . .	„ „ „ „ „ „ „ .	„
64	Bikaner . .	Sculpture from Pallu. Now in the Fort of Bikaner . .	„
65	„ . .	Marble frame from Pallu. Now in the Fort of Bikaner .	„
66	„ . .	„ „ „ „ „ „ „ „ .	„
67	„ . .	„ „ „ „ „ „ „ „ .	„
68	„ . .	„ „ „ „ „ „ „ „ .	„
69	„ . .	Frame with back piece for idol from Pallu. Now in the Fort of Bikaner.	
70	Hanoomangarh	The Fort	„
71	„	„	„
72	„	The exterior of the Fort	„
73	Suratgarh .	Moulded brick from Suratgarh (Rangmahall) . . .	$6\frac{1}{2}\times4\frac{3}{4}$
74	„ .	„ „ „ „ . . .	„
75	„ .	„ „ „ „ . . .	„
76	„ .	„ „ „ „ . . .	„
77	„ .	„ „ „ „ . . .	„
78	„ .	„ „ „ „ . . .	„
79	„ .	„ „ „ „ . . .	„
80	„ .	„ „ „ „ . . .	„
81	„ .	„ „ „ „ . . .	„

APPENDIX D—*contd.*

No.	Place and District.	Description.	Size.
82	Suratgarh .	Moulded brick from Suratgarh (Rangmahall) . . .	6½ × 4½
83	" .	" " " " . . .	8½ × 6½
84	" .	" " " " . . .	6½ × 4½
85	" .	" " " " . . .	"
86	" .	" " " " . . .	"
87	" .	" " " " . . .	"
88	" .	" " " " . . .	"
89	" .	" " " " . . .	"
90	" .	" " " " . . .	"
91	" .	" " " " . . .	8½ × 6½
92	" .	" " " " . . .	6½ × 4½
93	" .	" " " " . . .	"
94	" .	Terracotta from Suratgarh (Rangmahall)	8½ × 6½
95	" .	" " "	6½ × 4½
96	" .	" " "	"
97	Bikaner . .	Terracottas from Rangmahall, now in the Fort of Bikaner .	8½ × 6½
98	" . .	" " " " .	6½ × 4½
99	" . .	Moulded brick from Rangmahall, now in the Fort of Bikaner	"
100	" . .	Terracotta from Vadopala	8½ × 6½
101	" . .	" "	"
102	" . .	" "	"
103	" . .	" "	"
104	" . .	" "	6½ × 4½
105	" . .	" "	8½ × 6½
106	" . .	Moulded brick from Vadopala	"
107	Kalibanga .	Vases and other relics found in a cinerary urn at Kalibanga .	"
108	" . .	Clay relics from Kalibanga	"
109	" . .	Terracotta figurine from Kalibanga	6½ × 4½

APPENDIX D—*contd.*

No.	Place and District.	Description.	Size.
110	Ratangarh .	Loose sculpture from Ladasara, now in the Fort of Ratangarh	6½×4¾
111	Ladasara .	Loose sculpture	8½×6½
		PUNJAB.	
112	Taxila—Chir tope (Rawalpindi District).	Dharmarajika Stupa. General view from East-North-East .	"
113	"	" " " " North . .	"
114	"	" " Fragment of stone slab No. 123 .	"
115	"	" " Gandhara bracket No. 97 . .	"
116	"	" " " " " . .	"
117	"	" " " fragments Nos. 27, 109 and 124	"
118	"	Dhyani Buddha and two attendants	"
119	"	Lid of Steatite relic casket No. 98 and Denlil . . .	"
120	"	Hanging lamp No. 160	6½×4¾
121	"	Stucco heads Nos. 62 and 188	8½×6½
122	"	Terracotta bull and a baked clay whistle No. 48 and 66 .	"
123	"	Gold and copper objects Nos. 135, 42, 178, 1 and 141 . .	"
124	"	Copper objects Nos. 146, 117, 138, 94 and 100 . . .	"
125-127	Taxila—Jaulian (Hazara District).	Panoramic view of the Haro valley seen from South from the top of the main stupa.	"
128	"	Bodhisattva Maitreya on the East face of the stupa A 11 .	"
129	"	The two colossal Buddhas on the South-West corner of the main stupa with smaller seated Buddhas in between .	"
130	"	The female worshipper on the South-East corner of Stupa A 15.	"
131	"	The three seated Buddhas on the east face of stupa A 15, with a continuous Kharoshthi inscription on their pedestal.	"
132	"	The two lowermost tiers on the north face of stupa A. 16 .	"
133	"	The two lowermost tiers on the south face of stupa A 16 .	"

Appendix D—*contd.*

No.	Place and District.	Description.	Size.
134	Taxila—Jaulian (Hazara District).	The well preserved acanthus capital on the west face of stupa A 16	$8\frac{1}{2}\times6\frac{1}{2}$
135	”	The headless standing Buddhas and the smaller seated Buddha on the west half of the front face of the main stupa	”
136	”	The headless standing Buddhas and the smaller seated Buddha on the west half of the front face of the main stupa	
137	”	The inscribed seated Buddha on the east half of the front face of the main stupa	”
138	”	The highly ornamented Bodhisattva on the west face of stupa D 1	”
139	”	The Buddha and Bodhisattva figures in niches supported by Lions and Elephants on the west face of stupa D 1 .	”
140	”	The Atlas holding wine jar and double handled cantharus on the east face of stupa D.	$6\frac{1}{2}\times4\frac{1}{2}$
141	”	The niche containing seated Buddha with two female attendants holding spear and stupa on the north face of stupa D 4	$8\frac{1}{2}\times6\frac{1}{2}$
142-144	”	The three niches on the south-east corner of the second tier stupa D 4	”
145	”	The richly decorated Bodhisattva figure on the south face of the stupa	”
146	”	The richly decorated Bodhisattva figure on the south face of the stupa	”
147	”	Detailed view of stupa D 4 from south-east . . .	”
148	”	Pedestal with stucco decoration opposite to stupa A 13 .	”
149	”	The boldly executed lotus on the wall in front of chapel B 28.	”
150	”	The figures on the jambs and plinth of chapel C 34 . .	$6\frac{1}{2}\times4\frac{1}{2}$
151	”	The heavily ornamented Maitreya in chapel C 33 . .	$8\frac{1}{2}\times6\frac{1}{2}$
152	”	The throne and legs of colossal figures in the porch of chapel C 33	”
153	”	The small seated Buddha in the back wall of chapel C 19 .	$6\frac{1}{2}\times4\frac{1}{2}$
154	”	The three ladders in chapel C 15	”
155-157	”	The figures in niche to left of entrance of monastery . .	$8\frac{1}{2}\times6\frac{1}{2}$

APPENDIX D—*contd.*

No.	Place and District.	Description.	Size.
158	Taxila—Jaulian (Hazara District.)	A typical doorway of cell in the Monastery . . .	$6\frac{1}{2}\times4\frac{3}{4}$
159	"	" " " " " . . .	"
160	"	The niche in the front of cella 27	"
161	"	The fine Buddha (?) head in chapel in cell No. 8 . . .	"
162	"	Votive stupa of stucco	$8\frac{1}{2}\times6\frac{1}{2}$
163	"	Stucco head No. 57	"
164	"	" " 32	"
165	"	" " 171	"
166	"	" " 172	"
167	"	Terracotta and stucco heads Nos.	"
168	"	Stucco heads Nos. 110, 149 and 174	"
169	"	" " " 10, 50 and 168	"
170	"	" " " 160, 12, 174, 92 and 93	"
171	"	" " " 148, 161, 162 and 159	"
172	"	Stucco figures	"
173	"	Stucco heads Nos. 89, 91, 99, 90 and 4	"
174	"	6 stucco heads	"
175	"	8 " " Nos. 98, 186, 86, 123, 123, 90, 101 and 34 .	"
176	"	8 " "	"
177	"	11 " "	"
178	"	5 " " Nos. 179, 89, 18 and 23 and 143 . .	"
179	"	8 " " Nos. 168, 159, 186, 149, 114, 4, 171, and 64	"
180	"	Stucco figures in a niche	"
181	"	" " No. 192	"
182	"	One stucco and three terracotta heads, Nos. 89 and 197 .	"
183	"	Three stucco figures	"
184	"	Six stucco figures	"

APPENDIX D—*contd.*

No.	Place and District.	Description.	Size.
185	Ta̲ila Jaulian (Hazara District).	Stone sculpture Dhyani Buddha No. 1	8½ × 6½
186	,,	,, ,, Standing Buddha	,,
187	,,	,, fragments	,,
188	,,	,, seated Buddha	,,
189	,,	,, and terracotta objects	,,
190	,,	Earthen pot	6½ × 4¾
191	,,	Potteries Nos. 276, 247, 301 and 270	8½ × 6½
192	,,	,, Nos. 300, 302, 253, 278, 247 and 301	,,
193	,,	Copper objects Nos. 125, 124, 68, 1, 120, 4, 313 and 126	,,
194	,,	,, ,, Nos. 231, 224, 234 and 334	,,
195	,,	One seated Buddha one tripod and a finial	,,
196	,,	Copper caskets Nos. 224 and 231	6½ × 4¾
197	,,	,, bell and two other objects	8½ × 6½
198	,,	,, objects	,,
199	,,	8 Iron objects	,,
200	,,	7 ,,	,,
201	,,	10 ,,	,,
202	Kunala Monastery (Rawalpindi District).	Kunala Monastery from South-West	,,
203	,,	,, ,, ,, North-West	,,
204	,,	Detail view of the wall at the foot of the hill	,,
205	,,	Stone Chiragh and a copper object No. 73 and 46	6½ × 4¾
206	,,	Lower portion of a stone Casket	,,
207	,, and Sirkap (Rawalpindi District).	Iron object S. K. 678 and 90 and K. M. 45	,,
208	,,	Copper objects S.K. 393, 447 and 728 and K.M. 72	,,
209	,,	Iron objects, S.K. 140, 108, K.M. 81, 35, 90 and 135	8½ × 6½

APPENDIX D—*concld.*

No.	Place and District.	Description.	Size.
210	Taxila Kunala Monastery and Sirkap (Rawalpindi District).	Stucco fragments Nos. S. K. 772 and 404, K.M. 98 . .	8½×6½
211	Sirkap . .	" " Nos. S. K. 820	"
212	" . .	Copper dish and a copper mirror	"
213	" . .	Ivory handles of mirror, bone object, and lid of stone casket	6½×4½
214	" . .	Terracotta head No. 73, Glass bead 474 Glass object 592, Lower portion of a casket 551 and stone object 65 . .	"
215	" . .	Copper pot and a copper tube Nos. 164 and 37 . . .	"
216	" . .	Earthen dish	"
217	" . .	Gold bracelet	"
218	" . .	"	"
219	Sanchi . .	Tope I, General view from N.-N.-E.	8½×6½
220	" . .	Duplicate of 219	"
221	" . .	East Gate	"
222	" . .	Bodhisattva with Vasishka's inscription on pedestal . .	"
223	" . .	Tope II, ground railing, top medallion of a pillar . .	"
224	Miscellaneous .	Impression of a Brahmi inscription	"
225	"	Buddha seated in Dhyan mudra	"
226	"	Duplicate of 225	"
227	Sanchi (Bhopal State).	Tope I, South gate, (West pillar inner face) worship of Tatagatha's hair and head dress	"
228	Ajanta (Hyderabad).	Cave No. XVII, all of antechamber questions of Sariputra .	"

APPENDIX E.

Report of the Archæological Section, Indian Museum.

(BY SIR JOHN MARSHALL.)

Establishment.—Dr. D. B. Spooner, Superintendent, Archæological Survey, Eastern Circle, remained my deputy holding charge of the Archæological Section up to the 19th June, when he left for Simla to officiate for me as Director-General of Archæology, after duly handing it over to M. C. Duroiselle, who acted for him in the Eastern Circle. This arrangement, however, had to be changed in the month following. The services of Mr. D. R. Bhandarkar, M.A., Superintendent, Archæological Survey, Western Circle, were lent by the Government of India to the Calcutta University in the capacity of Carmichael Professor of Ancient Indian History and Culture, and at my suggestion it was also decided that he should be placed in charge of the Archæological Section, Indian Museum, in order that it might be brought into direct touch with the teaching of Indian History. When Prof. Bhandarkar came to Calcutta, he was therefore made my deputy in that Section, and he took charge of the same from M. Duroiselle on the 16th July. On the same day the Professor took charge also of the Assistant Superintendentship of the Section from Mr. R. D. Banerji, M.A., who succeeded him in the Western Circle. The post held by the latter in the Museum and that of the Gallery Assistant by Pandit B. B. Bidyabinoda were by Government orders held in abeyance, and in lieu thereof two temporary posts of Assistant Curators were created. To one of these Pandit Bidyabinoda was promoted, and for the other was selected Maulavi A. M. J. Muhammad from the office of the Archæological Survey, Eastern Circle.

Mr. Percy Brown, A.R.C.A., Principal, Government School of Art, Calcutta, continued to be the Exhibition Officer as last year.

Leave.—Babu B. C. Mukherji, Clerk, was absent on privilege leave from the 23rd July to 5th September, and a substitute was taken for the period.

Library.—156 books were added to the Library. Thirty-four only were purchased, and the rest are presentations.

Photographs.—1,416 photographic prints were received during the year from the different Circles of the Archæological Survey and from my office. Above two thousand prints were mounted in albums by the Markman.

Galleries.—Under my instructions Mr. Percy Brown, the Exhibition Officer, re-arranged the Bharhut room. Those fragments of the Bharhut rail which were in the Gupta Gallery were removed to, and exhibited in, the Bharhut room. Some plaster exhibits in the same room were duly repaired.

(*b*) In the new gallery some pre-historic iron articles and tiles of the Muhammadan period were exhibited.

(*c*) Some of the exhibits in the Bharhut, Gandhara and new galleries have been labelled in gold letters on black-polished wooden boards.

Owing to the ill-health of Mr. Percy Brown, the furnishing of the new gallery was not completed, and the same could not be opened this year.

(*d*) In accordance with the suggestion of the Trustees of the Indian Museum to all its Sections—I appointed Pandit B. B. Bidyabinoda, Assistant Curator, as Guide in the Archæological gallery, and he has been working in this connection since 22nd August for two days in the week. People, especially the educated section of the public, eagerly listen to his lectures, and it seems that the idea of appointing a guide is being appreciated by the public.

(*e*) To arrest the disintegration of some of the antiquities in the gallery, I deputed my Archæological Chemist, Mr. Sana Ullah, B.A., M.Sc., F.C.S., to the Museum immediately after his arrival from England, *i.e.*, in July last. He has been provided with a chemical laboratory for this purpose. The number of objects conserved by him so far, *i.e.*, up to 31st March 1918, are as follows :—

1. Khotan Manuscript . . . . 11 leaves.

After his treatment the manuscript pages were readable, and Prof. Bhandarkar is now engaged upon deciphering them with the help of Pandit B. B. Bidyabinoda. They are in Gupta character of the 5th and 6th century A.D.

2. Clay, terracotta and stucco 80
3. Iron 42
4. Lead 9
5. Silver 58

On arrival at the Museum he found that the objects of clay, terracotta and stucco were suffering. Consequently these were taken up first. There are also visible signs of deterior-

APPENDIX E—*concld.*

ation in some of the stone and metallic antiquities, which will be taken in hand in due course.

Coin Room.—Mr. R. D. Banerji continued to be the Assistant Superintendent till the 15th July, and remained in charge of the Coin Room. As he was thereafter badly wanted in the Western Circle to which he had been transferred, it was not possible to make over charge of the Coin Room to Prof. Bhandarkar in that month. About the middle of October he returned to Calcutta for this purpose, with the permission of the Bombay Government. Till then the Coin Room had been securely locked and sealed. Final charge of the Coin Room was taken over by Prof. Bhandarkar on the 1st March.

Tour.—In the month of June Mr. R. D. Banerji went on tour under my orders to Bhubaneswar, Puri and Konarak for some iconographical and epigraphical work.

In the middle of the month of March Prof. Bhandarkar, at my suggestion, went to Chitorgarh in Rajputana in connection with his monographs on the celebrated Kirtistambha there.

New accessions.—The following additions were made to the Archæological Collections :—

(i) *Inscriptions.*—Two bricks inscribed with Cuneiform character from Mesopotamia presented by Mr. A. M. Stewart, P. W. Inspector, Mesopotamia Railway. They have been sent for decipherment to Mr. A. H. Harley, M.A., Principal, Calcutta Madrassa.

(ii) *Coins.*—Altogether 653 coins were added to the Cabinet during the year—86 gold, 303 silver, 255 copper and 9 billon. Out of these 449 coins were purchased, and the rest received as presentations from the Jodhpur and Gwalior States, Madras, Central Provinces and United Provinces Governments.

A classified list of coins added to the Cabinet is given below :—

Class.	Gold.	Silver.	Copper.	Billon.
Native State	...	190	244	...
Nepal	...	...	1	...
South Indian	84	...	4	...
Sassanian of Persia	...	2	...	...
East Indian	1	...	...	...
Burmese (Symbolical)	...	6	...	...
Kashmir	...	...	1	...
Sharqi	...	...	2	...
Afghan	...	2	1	...
Mughal	...	99	1	...
Turki (Slave)	...	...	...	9
Kabul	...	3	...	...
Mysur (Hyder Ali)	1	...	...	...
Suri	...	...	1	...
Oudh	...	1	...	...
TOTAL	86	303	255	9

J. H. MARSHALL,
Director General of Archæology.

SGPI—S 14—38DGArch.—1-5-20.